WAY OF THE
JAFA

WAY OF THE
JAFA

The guide to surviving Auckland and Aucklanders

Lee Baker

with Benjamin Crellin

WARNING: Some content may offend. Parental guidance advised.

National Library of New Zealand Cataloguing-in-Publication Data

Baker, Lee Anthony.
Way of the JAFA : the guide to surviving Auckland and
Aucklanders / Lee Baker with Benjamin Crellin. 1st ed.
ISBN 1-86958-989-0
1. Auckland (N.Z.)—Social life and customs—Humor.
2. Auckland (N.Z.)—Description and travel—Humor.
I. Crellin, Benjamin. II. Title.
307.5099324—dc 22

Published in 2004 by Hodder Moa Beckett Publishers Ltd
[a member of the Hodder Headline Group]
4 Whetu Place, Mairangi Bay
Auckland, New Zealand

Photographs by Lee Baker and Kevyn Male
Designed and produced by Hodder Moa Beckett Publishers Ltd
Printed by Tien Wah Press

CONTENTS

ACKNOWLEDGEMENTS

Thanks must first go to Warren and Kevin at Hodder Moa Beckett for taking a punt on two strangers with an idea. Many thanks are due to David Downs, the man who first suggested the idea of turning our ideas into a book and whom remained generous with his time and advice throughout. Very special thanks to Paul Yates who, as editor, contributed some sparkling morsels of material not to mention input and guidance of a calibre few others could offer. Thanks also to editors Jane Hingston and Cara Torrance and to designer Craig Violich. Extra special thanks to Linda McFetridge and Jake Morrison for giving so generously of their time and for their constant support. Special thanks also to Christina Read and Jason Dufty for their illustrations at such short notice. Much gratitude to the following fine people and businesses for their support and assistance: Jodie Molloy, Nic Romaniuk, Brendhan Lovegrove, Nigel McCulloch, Cory Matthews, Dion Matthews, Wendy Matthews, Kevin Molloy, Jonathan Brugh, Jacqui Loates, Mike Dean, Jim and Miranda at First Scene, Brendan Perkins, Lisa Baker, Barbarina Baker, Daniel Perkins, Maree Bishop, Ken Bishop, Amy West, Edmund McWilliams, Toby McWilliams, Jonathan Brown, Jemaine Clement, Michael Keating, Julie Nolan, Raybon Kan, Brett Stewart, Jason White, Ryan Hutchings, Jarrod Holt, Scott Blanks, Mike Loder, Jason Smith, Gemma Ross, Jackie Van Beek, Adam Gardiner, Leigh Warn, Les Mills World of Fitness, Dominic Bowden, Roxy Birch, Cinde Custer, Zeb from Cityboards, Smiley from Sponge, Mark Wilson, Chippy Wilson, Shannon Wilson, Max Wilson, Mary from Citymix, Clayton Whiddett and Shanelle Stephen from Team McMillan, Greg Brinck and Mark Wilson from Independent Prestige Ltd, Ace Motors LMVD, Anna-Lena Kraus, Masud Milas, Adam Kinmond, Rügen Du Bray, Stagecoach, Taro Teppan-Yaki, Robert Smallridge, Jonny McArthur and Jackie Strang at SPQR, Lauren Dirksen, Zoë Howes, Olivia Howes and the Crellin family.

Lee Baker & Benjamin Crellin

HOW TO USE THIS BOOK

Stand with your legs apart at about the width of your shoulders. Hold the book in front of you at about chest height. Open the book to a selected page and begin reading. Read from left to right at first using both your eyes and being careful to maintain an even pace. Be sure to observe all punctuation and grammar.

If you're using this book whilst still in the bookstore, occasionally laugh audibly, point at favourite pages and say things like, 'That's *very* funny!' or 'So true!' Then look at the price tag and exclaim, 'Wow, only $19.95! — I'd pay twice that for a book this good!' If such behaviour is embarrassing to you, you are clearly not a Jafa and therefore you need this book.

Now either put the book back on the shelf (BEING CAREFUL TO PLACE IT EXACTLY WHERE YOU FOUND IT) or proceed to the checkout and buy the book using an approved method of payment.

Do not under any circumstances attempt to steal this book. If you are thinking about stealing this book, you need to take a good long look at yourself, mate.

ABOUT THIS BOOK

This book is an ingenious combination of a city guide and a 'how to' survival guide. Because this is the first time anyone has attempted such a risky fusion there are some inherent dangers that the reader should be aware of. One is that the book may make no sense at all. To reduce the likelihood of this, **bold text** has been used to make information clearer and more accessible, and also because it makes things look quite professional*. For ease of use it has been written in plain, easy to understand English (except where an inability to write has caused us to lapse into unintelligible rambling). Everything else should be self-explanatory. That's the point.

WHAT TO DO IF YOU DON'T LIKE THIS BOOK

If you find you don't like this book, the first thing you must do is stop blaming yourself. It's not your fault you don't understand highly cultured literature. The good news is that not liking something is a matter of opinion. Opinions can be changed because they are only mindsets. If you think you may not like this book all you have to do is **choose** to like it and your problem is solved. (See what we mean about the bold text? It really makes a difference.)

---

* By the way, we'll also be using these tiny asterisks to denote footnotes because these look even more professional than bold text.

WHAT TO DO IF THIS BOOK WAS AN UNWANTED GIFT

This can be a serious problem. It's not a matter of liking or not liking the book, you'd just rather have the money. We understand. After all, isn't a gift supposed to be about *your* happiness? Exactly, and yet it would be rude to ask the giver to take it back — this would imply they made a mistake or that you don't appreciate the thought. Act quickly. Ask when and where this book was bought. Disguise the nature of your inquiry by saying something like, 'I thought I saw you there buying a book. Fancy that!' Now you know the date of purchase, gain access to the gift-giver's bank account statement pertaining to the day of purchase. Make a photocopy of this. Go to the store where the book was purchased and, using the photocopy in lieu of a receipt, demand a cash refund. DO NOT accept an offer of credit — you'll probably give in to the temptation to buy the latest issue of *Who Weekly*, and eventually lose the credit slip. Insist on cash (it's not like they haven't got any). Once you have the cash you can spend it on something useful, such as one of those chilly-bins that has an AM/FM radio built into it.

OTHER USES FOR *WAY OF THE JAFA*

This book can also be used to:
- Slap the dog;
- Maim the cat;
- Open a can (may take some time);
- Start a fire (requires two copies to rub together);
- Start a conversation (introduce a friend to the book);
- End a conversation (introduce the book to a friend);
- Preserve flowers or butterflies;
- Construct a house using a revolutionary new material (i.e. this book);
- Act as a bookmark for a much larger book.

INTRODUCTION TO THIS BOOK

It is a rare state of affairs for a developed country to have just one city that towers above all others as the pulsing heart of its culture, the bustling commercial centre of the nation and as a dazzling metropolis on the world stage. Little wonder then that New Zealand has no such city and has had to make do with Auckland.

The City of Sails is New Zealand's biggest city and undoubtedly the most exciting of Australia's suburbs. Auckland is unquestionably the first choice for any New Zealander who hasn't been able to make it overseas. It attracts more tourists, migrants and overstayers than any other centre. It consistently emerges as New Zealand's clear leader in all areas: sport, culture, traffic congestion, crime — the list goes on. Internationally, Auckland continues to set the standard for cities built on an isthmus. But it wasn't always this way. Many New Zealanders might be surprised to know that Auckland was once a dull city with very little to recommend it beyond its easily pronounceable name. However, thanks to an increasing number of major events such as the America's Cup, the Auckland property boom and the P-epidemic, Auckland is now a fast-moving and vibrant urban centre.

There is no doubt that Auckland, like any major city, faces a number of problems. Environmental issues are the most pressing concern. Emission controls were introduced in the central city after it was found that Auckland's air contained levels of pretension in excess of World Health Organization recommended limits. But the response at a local level has been rigorous. The Auckland City Council has led the way by initiating several highly innovative development projects, and then shelving them due to cost. Thanks to the Council's superb leadership Aucklanders can continue to look forward to a wide range of improvements around the city as they will never happen.

Ultimately, then, it falls to the people of Auckland to make their city a better place to raise children and house prices. Historically, Aucklanders have never shrunk from this challenge. Refusing to let a crippling lack of real culture impede them, they have managed to turn this very lack of culture into a cultural phenomenon unto itself. The people of Auckland have transformed what would otherwise be a sprawling, lifeless place with no real heart into a city that can hold its head up high as probably the world's best stopover on the way to the South Island. In so doing Aucklanders have distinguished themselves as their own social species — affectionately called **Jafas**. But what precisely are Jafas? Apart from their large petrol-guzzling four-wheel-drive cars, what drives them? What makes them tick? *Way of the Jafa* represents the first and quite possibly the last attempt to answer these and other important questions. Inside you will find a complete guide to being an Aucklander. It will help you not only survive the city but also enjoy Auckland for everything it has to offer, from its stunningly tall Sky Tower to its stunningly tall transvestite prostitutes.

1 DEFINING THE JAFA
WHAT IS A JAFA?

WHAT IS A JAFA?

The origin and meaning of the term 'Jafa' is the source of much debate. This affectionate moniker is derived from an acronym that is considered to have several possible meanings.

SOME MEANINGS FOR THE ACRONYM JAFA

Just Another Friendly Aucklander
Just Another Fun Aucklander
Just Another Fantastic Aucklander
Just Another Forced Acronym
Jesus Always Favours Aucklanders
Jamaican Anglers' and Fishermen's Association.

WAY OF THE JAFA

THE NATURE OF THE JAFA

Regardless of its precise meaning, the term 'Jafa' is now synonymous with Aucklanders and their many peculiarities. The Jafa's manner has been described as somewhere between **aloof** and untouchable. This is a little unkind because a Jafa is really no more aloof than any other extremely aloof New Zealander. Jafas are often depicted as being pretentious, arrogant and overly concerned with the possession and exhibition of material wealth. However, they possess many other positive qualities, too.

Jeff the Jafa says:
'Auckland is far more important than the rest of the country and everyone knows it. Why else would we have our own nationally recognised acronym?'

Visitors to Auckland report that Jafas are friendly and helpful, particularly when it comes to helping them spend their money. They possess an impressive general knowledge about their city and may even be aware of the rest of New Zealand. Recent research suggests Jafas have a much better awareness of their place in the world than is generally acknowledged, as the map opposite shows.

Jafas are especially helpful when giving directions, often you don't even have to ask.

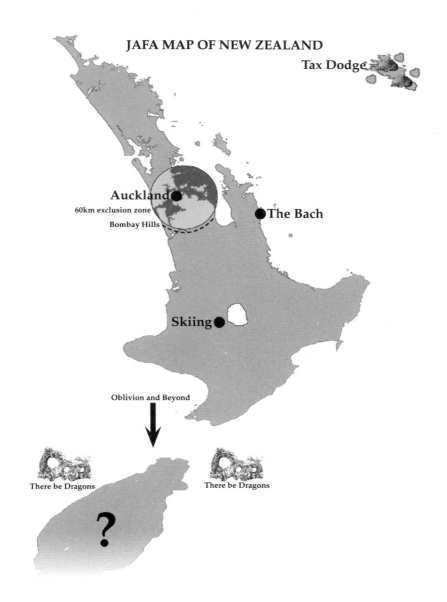

JAFA MAP OF NEW ZEALAND

Tax Dodge

Auckland

60km exclusion zone

Bombay Hills

The Bach

Skiing

Oblivion and Beyond

There be Dragons

There be Dragons

?

WAY OF THE JAFA

ARE JAFAS GENETICALLY DISTINCT?

For several years now scientists have been searching for the **Jafa gene**. Thanks to the *Inhuman Genome Project*, a scientific think tank dedicated to documenting genetic anomalies in human DNA, the gene that makes Aucklanders special has finally been uncovered. It was not hard to isolate the Jafa gene because other genes proved to be 'molecularly disinclined' to interact with it. Scientists noted that the Jafa gene appeared to have nothing in common with other genes occurring in the New Zealand gene pool. This has not stopped natural selection resulting in the Jafa gene becoming the dominant gene in almost a third of New Zealanders. Advancements in gene therapy mean there is now hope that the Jafa gene can be removed from the gene pool and, if necessary, destroyed.

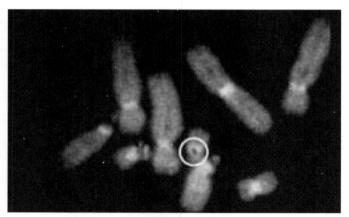

The Jafa gene, seen here with friends, is dominant in almost a third of New Zealanders.

ARE YOU A JAFA?

Even if you were not born or raised in Auckland you may have acquired some Jafa traits simply as a result of being in contact with Jafas. Indeed, you may already have developed some of the characteristics that will help you live life according to the *Way of the Jafa*. To test your Jafa level of sophistication, take the following easy test to determine your JQ (Jafa Quotient).

Defining the Jafa

JAFA QUOTIENT ASSESSMENT TEST

1. A 'Frappucino' is:
    a. A type of coffee you're happy to pay $4 for because it sounds Italian
    b. Al Pacino's younger brother
    c. Italian slang for a woman's reproductive organs
2. What is a 'vegan'?
    a. Someone for whom malnutrition is a lifestyle choice
    b. A descendent of Sir Thomas Vegan, the first man to successfully climb Mount Eden without the aid of a packed lunch
    c. A breed of dog that should probably be banned, according to talkback radio
    d. A member of the same race as Dr Spock
3. Is your cellphone the size of:
    a. An average cellphone
    b. A smaller than average cellphone
    c. A matchbox
    d. You're not sure because you inhaled it
4. Wellington is located in:
    a. The North Island
    b. The South Island
    c. Who cares?
5. What is a 'disabled park'?
    a. A car park provided for disabled motorists
    b. A car park with a car in it
    c. A playground where all the swings have been broken by obese children
6. What is the first rule of buying real estate?
    a. Location
    b. Location
    c. Location
    d. All of the above
7. What is the little gearstick next to the big gearstick inside your Jeep?
    a. An emergency back-up lever for the big gearstick
    b. A design fault
    c. Proof that gearsticks sometimes breed
8. What is a 'Fluffy'?
    a. A frothy milk espresso drink for kids which costs 50 cents in Papakura but $4.50 in Ponsonby
    b. A hirsute woman
    c. A person whose job it is to keep male actors aroused between takes on an adult film
9. Why should you never leave your drink unattended in an Auckland bar?
    a. Because it might get lonely
    b. Because someone might turn it into an anaesthetic while you're in the toilet
    c. Because, even though it's just a bottle of local beer, it cost you $9 so you can't afford to lose it

10. Gucci, Versace and Armani are:
    a. Venereal diseases
    b. The Three Tenors
    c. The front row of the Italian rugby team
    d. Two-thirds of your income for one-tenth of your wardrobe

11. If someone describes himself as a barista, he is:
    a. Trying to justify his crap job as a coffee waiter with a ridiculous job title
    b. A lawyer who can't spell
    c. An Italian version of 'Barry' and probably an all right bloke

12. What is a 4X4?
    a. The best way to get toddlers up the steep part of Parnell Rise
    b. 16
    c. A sex act involving four men and four women

13. You meet a backpacker at a party who tells you she is looking forward to visiting the Mainland and wants your recommendations. Do you:
    a. Make a list of your favourite South Island spots for her
    b. Recommend that place where Brad Pitt and Jennifer Aniston apparently stayed
    c. Ask her why she is going to visit a brand of cheese

14. What is the foreshore?
    a. Another way Americans say 'Yes'
    b. The only part of your million-dollar coastal property that was free
    c. Something that belongs equally to all New Zealanders, but more equally to Maori
    d. An issue of customary rights, such as the customary right of Pakeha to ignore the customary rights of Maori

15. What does SUV stand for?
    a. Sports Utility Vehicle
    b. Severely Under-utilized Vehicle
    c. Sorry U-can't-afford-this Vehicle

16. What does 'Gore' mean to you?
    a. Blood and guts and things like that
    b. A delightful South Island hamlet
    c. A delightful South Island hamlet renowned for its blood and guts and things like that

17. Which consonant would you use to replace the 'A' from Auckland in order to create a name that better describes the city?
    a. F
    b. S
    c. You wouldn't because that would be disrespectful to New Zealand's most important city and anyway you don't appreciate this kind of idiotic, juvenile humour

18. What is Mount Eden?
    a. A state-of-the-art correctional facility
    b. A simply lovely suburb full of absolutely gorgeous villas
    c. Where Adam and Eve went skiing

Defining the Jafa

19. As a young bride-to-be, you're very much looking forward to your wedding day. However, 48 hours before the big day a huge pimple forms on your forehead. Do you:
    a. Draw a smiley face around it to detract attention from it
    b. Apply make-up
    c. Apply make-up and book an emergency facial
    d. Apply make-up, book an emergency facial and get breast implants just to be sure
20. What are the 'Nippon Clip-ons'?
    a. An attachment for your mobile phone
    b. A marital aid that applies intense pressure to your nipples
    c. The side lanes added to the Auckland Harbour Bridge to make it easier for suicidal Jafas to jump off
21. Which of the following phrases best sums up Auckland?
    a. A pretentious, congested city full of complete wankers who think there is no life south of the Bombay Hills
    b. And I really mean it about the people; they are total pricks who let the rest of the country down
    c. A beautiful multicultural city full of friendly people, lovely beaches and some simply divine renovated villas

RESULTS GUIDE
15 or more correct: You are a Jafa.
10–15 correct: You are a learner Jafa or Jafa sympathiser.
Less than 10 correct: Retire to Invercargill immediately.

ANSWERS: 1) A, 2) A, 3) D, 4) C, 5) B, 6) D, 7) C, 8) A, 9) C, 10) A, 11) A, 12) A, 13) C, 14) D, 15) C, 16) B, 17) C, 18) C, 19) D, 20) C, 21) C

2 REMEMBERING THE JAFA
A BRIEF HISTORY OF JAFAS

THE BEGINNINGS OF AUCKLAND

Around 3500 years ago **Maori** mariners landed at present-day Auckland and in so doing became the first Jafas. They named the area 'Tamaki-makau-rau', meaning 'land refreshingly free of foreigners'. But it was not long before European explorers made contact with Maori, mainly by ending up in their stomachs. Surprisingly, this did not deter European settlement, the effects of which were both immediate and devastating. The introduction of non-native species such as possums, weasels and **seamen** ravaged the indigenous populations. Whalers began to frequent Auckland, bringing with them liquor. Alcohol soon became a problem, as there was rarely enough to go around.

Remembering the Jafa

William Hobson, the governor of New South Wales, was dispatched from Australia to assess the situation and report on whether Auckland could make a suitable capital for New Zealand. Hobson sent word to his superiors that the site of the proposed city was 'a lawless, Godless pit of poverty, despair and moral turpitude'. He added that it would make an ideal capital for the colony. But early efforts to found the city were stifled by civil unrest. Disgruntled Maori fought to repulse the British, fearing their exotic diseases and that they might be forced to watch cricket for days on end. Although Maori were noted warriors, revered for their courage, strong tackling and speed to the breakdown, the colonialists successfully repelled them using cannons, muskets and **syphilis**. The warring Maori are believed to have been the first to use the term 'Jafa' to describe Aucklanders — as an acronym for Just Another Foreign Aggressor.

When the Treaty of Waitangi was signed in 1840 the situation in Auckland calmed down and Maori ceded most of their territory. The prized islands of the Hauraki Gulf were not covered by the Treaty and would have remained with Maori had they not been lost in a card game two years later.

With the region finally under the control of one authority the task of building a city could begin. The early pioneers soon turned a wilderness of fern into a bustling centre with all the hallmarks of a colonial outpost — dusty store-lined streets, horse-drawn carts and whiskey-swilling whores. Before long Auckland had become New Zealand's biggest city — a development that historians now acknowledge forever changed its people and their relationship with the rest of the country.

Auckland's first house at Freeman's Bay. Originally built in 1831 for £3, this two-bedroom villa recently sold for $4.5 million.

THE GREAT FIRE OF AUCKLAND, 1820

Unlike the 'great fires' of other major cities such as the Great Fire of London (1666), the Great Inferno of Edinburgh (1538) or the Disco Inferno of New York (1977), the Great Fire of Auckland (1820) happened early in the town's history. The fire, which was started accidentally by an arsonist, devastated most of the city. However, as the city comprised only 15 canvas tents and a pigpen, it could have been worse. Certainly it was no great historic event and would hardly warrant a mention except that this space needed to be filled.

GREAT JAFAS FROM HISTORY

SAMUEL MARSDEN-POINT
(1765–1838)

Samuel Marsden-Point was Auckland's first and most prolific missionary (he held the record for the most number of conversions in a calendar year until it was broken by Grant Fox in 1990). A former altar boy, Marsden-Point arrived from Scotland in 1801 to spread the gospel. His teachings emphasised the importance of 'communal love' and 'sharing of body and soul, but mainly body' as he put it. He took his message to wayward Maori youth. A mission was set up at the site of present-day Karangahape Road and became famous as the first to offer so-called 'drive-thru' conversions. After months spent schooling his mainly female converts in the ways of the Lord, Marsden-Point began to appreciate the oral brilliance of Maori. He translated the language into English syntax and helped Maori create their own words to describe new Christian concepts such as 'the laying on of hands' (*pakeharoha*). Marsden-Point also had political ambitions and for a brief time the capital of New Zealand was a missionary position atop a hill. In 1964 Marsden-Point had an oil refinery named after him, then considered the highest honour bestowed in New Zealand.

KATE SHEPFORD (1848–1934)

Kate Shepford was the leading light of the early Auckland women's suffrage movement. She successfully campaigned for dresses that women could breathe in, lobbying hard against the Victorian women's clothing she believed imposed patriarchal ideals of beauty, not to mention internal organ damage. She achieved infamy by becoming the first woman to burn her corset as an act of protest. Unfortunately, she was wearing the corset at the time and the resulting burns nearly claimed her life. She marked her comeback by forming New Zealand's first all-girl brass band, Kate and the Suffragettes, but after a controversial national tour the group disbanded. Shepford then turned her back on protest music and returned to politics. In 1870 she formed the **Auckland Women's Temperance Union**, a group that would prove instrumental in winning for women the right to vote, and the right to enjoy sex (officially recognised in 1879).

SIR ROYSON MOYESWORTH (1820–1886)

Sir Royson Moyesworth was the first Auckland mayor to propose a harbour crossing linking Auckland's North Shore with the central city. Moyesworth envisioned a 'glass tunnel of mighty construction', which would allow commuters a view of the harbour's undersea life. The Auckland City Council rejected the idea because of its cost and because it was believed that the harbour was home to a taniwha. Moyesworth is considered the most visionary of Auckland's 19th-century mayors, if only because of his passion for hallucinogens. A Catholic priest, Moyesworth was a staunch advocate of natural herbal remedies including the potent *Fungiphallusentienta* (magic mushroom), which he often administered as communion at his parish.

Outside of town planning and curling, Moyesworth's real passion was Rugby Union. He refereed provincial games and was known for his use of the tuba instead of the more commonly favoured whistle. The mayor's most famous moment came whilst refereeing the first **Ranfurly Shield** match between Auckland and Canterbury. With five minutes left in the match Moyesworth claimed to see a vision of the Virgin Mary in an offside position. He awarded a penalty to Auckland and the resulting points secured the Shield for the home side. He would have three more visions of Our Lady before his death, once in a church, once in a field and once in a bathing suit.

DAME SYLVIA WORTHINGTON-TATE-WORTHINGTON-TATE-AGAIN (1793–1865)

Dame Sylvia was the epitome of the rugged, unflappable pioneering Jafa woman. She single-handedly (with the help of 300 local Maori) cleared a huge area of bush we now know as the suburb of **Remuera**. There she designed and built her own 'delightfully renovated house with indoor-outdoor flow and extensive views of the harbour' (she later subdivided the property and built townhouses, which she sold to whalers for a tidy profit). Dame Sylvia is commonly known as the 'Mother of Public Relations' for setting up what is believed to be the world's first PR firm, Worthington-Tate-Worthington-Tate-Again and Associates, in 1830. Her clients included Hone Heke, whose attacks on the flagpole at Waitangi, she convinced newspapers, were simply the result of 'over-zealous tree felling'. It was on Dame Sylvia's advice that Chief Te Rauparaha elected to have a full facial tattoo or 'moko' — a move which many say saved his career. Sadly her career was overshadowed by **New Zealand's biggest PR disaster**, the Treaty of Waitangi. Dame Sylvia managed to get chiefs to sign by telling them the document guaranteed equal Maori ownership of all New Zealand, a promise the government (and every government since) had no intention of keeping.

ARNOLD GRAHAM CAMPBELL, MBE (1872–1969)

Arnold Graham Campbell was an Auckland inventor who refused to let a lack of resources stand in the way of revolutionary thinking. A leading nuclear physicist, Campbell made the **first attempt to split the atom** using a particle accelerator made from nothing but an old beer crate and the wire from a woman's brassiere. The experiment was a failure. However, Campbell did succeed in inventing the world's first wireless brassiere. On four separate occasions Campbell was unable to split the atom, although he claimed to have succeeded in fracturing it — a major breakthrough many say paved the way for Ernest Rutherford's later triumphs. In 1916 Campbell was awarded the Nobel Prize for Trying.

KEY MOMENTS IN THE HISTORY OF AUCKLAND

1656 — First European contact made. Early explorers introduce Maori to exotic items such as silk, spices and contracts to play for English Rugby League teams.

1740 — First missionaries arrive to spread the word of God along with other catchy words like 'alcohol' and 'herpes'.

1826 — William Hobson creates Auckland's first property boom after obtaining most of the region in return for a quilt and two shiny buttons.

1840 — Treaty of Waitangi brought to region for signing by Auckland Maori chiefs. New Zealand becomes first country in the world to officially recognise its native people's right to be exploited.

1842 — Hone Heke thrills Auckland crowds on wood-chopping exhibition tour.

1842 — Auckland established as capital of New Zealand, narrowly heading off a late charge by Shirley.

1850 — First recorded act of political correctness sees the term 'minimum wage' introduced to replace terms such as 'native wage' or 'button wage'.

1862 — Maori Wars begin.

1863 — Halftime in Maori Wars.

WAY OF THE JAFA

1864 — Maori Wars begin again in earnest, with the townspeople of Earnest suffering heavy losses.

1903 — Auckland women first to win right to vote, nag.

1936 — Auckland children become first kids in New Zealand to get free milk in schools when each receives their own cow.

1942 — Thousands of visiting US servicemen descend on Auckland, leaving their mark on Jafa women with romance, chivalry and genital warts.

1943 — Japanese submarine slips in and out of Waitemata Harbour completely unnoticed.

1949 — Auckland Harbour Bridge construction begins.

1959 — Auckland Harbour Bridge finished.

1959 — Auckland Harbour Bridge repaired.

1959 — Diagonal crossing at major intersections conceived as a way to encourage Aucklanders to mix.

1959 — First motorway completed.

1959 — First traffic jam.

1962 — First traffic jam cleared.

1977 — Raging Auckland feminists burn down an entire bra factory in Mount Roskill.

1981 — Anti-tour protests. Cliff Richard tour eventually cancelled.

1984 — Queen Street riots carry out much-needed revamp of Auckland's central business district.

1987 — Jafas lose millions in stock market crash, resulting in city-wide cutbacks of everything except hair.

1991 — Auckland police take possession of new 'American'-sounding sirens, said to be much cooler than the old-style ones.

1995 — The inaugural Devonport Wine Festival is held.

1996 — Devonport Wine Festival relaunched as Devonport Wine *and Food* Festival on recommendation of local police.

1996 — Sky City Casino opening hailed as a huge success with punters losing millions on the first night alone.

1997 — Sky Tower opens. Immediately acknowledged as the Southern Hemisphere's pointiest landmark.

1999 — Aerial spraying fails to improve West Auckland.

Remembering the Jafa

2000 — Team New Zealand successfully defends America's Cup against shoe and handbag magnate.

2000 — US President Bill Clinton visits Auckland, praises availability of cigars, women.

2003 — Second America's Cup defence sees NZL82 highlight the importance of water-safety skills for yachties.

2003 — P-epidemic grips Auckland, newsreaders.

2003 — Britomart Station opened.

2004 — Britomart Station welcomes its 100th commuter.

3 PLACING THE JAFA
AUCKLAND, CENTRE OF JAFADOM

GEOGRAPHY

Auckland is situated on an **isthmus**, which, at its narrowest point, is only 1 km wide. This explains everything from Auckland's mercurial weather to the character of the city. With such a narrow strip of land at its centre, much of the heat and energy normally retained by a landmass is dissipated into the sea causing the city to feel **lifeless and dull** — a common complaint of visitors. Even the many volcanoes that dot the city are referred to as 'dormant'. The greater Auckland area spreads 30 km to the East, 30 km to the West, as far north as it pleases and as far south as the Bombay Hills where it abruptly stops, at least psychologically.

POPULATION

Auckland's population is roughly 1.12 million. This is just short of the 1.25 million recommended by UNESCO as being necessary to create a city 'no more boring than Bill Gates'. Despite this obvious disadvantage Auckland still stakes a claim to being one of Australasia's most exciting cities (if you don't include Sydney, Melbourne, Brisbane, Adelaide, Perth, Nadi and Apia). Auckland's population density varies from low in the central suburbs to high in areas such as West Auckland where the population is remarkably dense. Statisticians tell us the city's population is increasing 'naturally' but is also affected by immigration, which besides increasing numbers enriches Auckland's ethnic profile and **taxi service**. Experts predict Auckland's population will be 2 million by the year 2050. Unfortunately, the hole in the ozone layer will be so big by then the city is expected to be uninhabitable, except possibly by genetically modified mutant cockroaches.

CULTURE

Due to a severe shortage, Auckland has had to import 100 per cent of its culture. This has come mainly from overseas and primarily from Polynesia. Auckland is now proud to be **the biggest Polynesian city in the world** and challenges all other cities to equal or better this.

ETHNIC PROFILE

The last census revealed just what a multicultural place Auckland has become. The city's ethnic breakdown is delineated along the following lines:

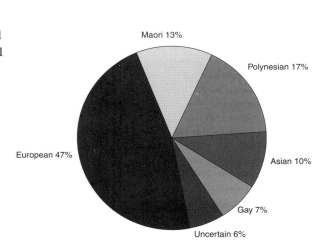

Maori 13%

Polynesian 17%

European 47%

Asian 10%

Gay 7%

Uncertain 6%

WAY OF THE JAFA

The biggest surprise of the last census results was the marked increase in Jafas of 'uncertain' descent, indicating increased integration of the population. The numbers of uncertains have grown steadily since 1900 with ever-increasing numbers of people who don't know who they are. Aucklanders of uncertain descent congregate in no particular precinct where they may or may not practise their ambiguous traditions and rituals in no particular organised fashion.

RELIGION

Christianity remains the most observed faith among Jafas. Most observe it from afar. Many Jafas will, however, celebrate Christian feast days such as Christmas, Easter and indeed any religious feast day that means a day off work. Auckland's religious profile has been greatly enriched by the city's many immigrants. Its spiritual spectrum now takes in everyone from those who believe in Jesus Christ to those who believe those who believe in Jesus Christ should be killed and those who don't believe in any God until they're diagnosed with cancer.

NINE MOST POPULAR JAFA BELIEF SYSTEMS

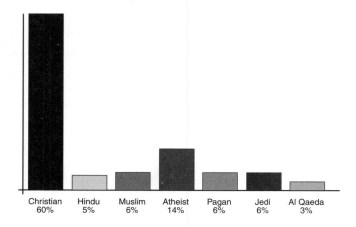

Christian	Hindu	Muslim	Atheist	Pagan	Jedi	Al Qaeda
60%	5%	6%	14%	6%	6%	3%

FLORA AND FAUNA

Auckland is rich in naturally occurring **concrete**, the building material that gives the city its famous bland look. The central business district is not, however, without its native wildlife, which includes hedgehogs, rats and **winos**.

ARCHITECTURE

Auckland is world renowned for its classical late-1980s architecture. It features some of the world's best examples of **faceless glass buildings**, some dating back as far as 15 years. Jafas have always been conscious of knocking down historic and otherwise discontemporaneous buildings to make way for square blocks that are much more cost-effective and attention-grabbing. As a result, Auckland's cityscape represents a delightful balance between the new, the not so new and building sites.

Many people fondly comment that Auckland resembles
a much smaller and blander version of Sydney.

CLIMATE

Auckland is famous for its **cancerously sunny** spells, chilling wind gusts and **horizontal rain** — often all in the same day. While most of New Zealand is considered to be temperate, Auckland is better described as 'temperamental'. This can make the city difficult to dress for or live in. The hole in the ozone layer affects UV-ray levels over the North Island and in summer Auckland's daily radiation levels are second only to Chernobyl's. On the plus side, you can get an all-over tan in the time it takes to say 'melanoma'.

CRIME AND OTHER PROBLEMS

Few people can live in Auckland long or even visit without expecting to have some experience of the city's crime problem. Street offending is a leading concern, particularly in the central city where offenders work in groups. Christians and Hari Krishnas are the worst. The latter have been known to subject their victims to traumatising percussive 'music'. The installation of security cameras in the central city area has been a big success. Although the number of violent attacks is yet to drop, the footage from these cameras has been sold to overseas Reality Television shows and earned rave reviews.

The growth of **gangs** is probably Auckland's most serious issue. Groups with social and cultural affiliations have formed various 'Mafia', which have recruited from the city's unemployed to create **disorganised crime syndicates**. With the increase in Asian immigrants, Asian crime syndicates have become a problem. The **triads** have been linked to a number of drive-by shootings in the city. However, in a landmark case of 2001, defence lawyers for the triads successfully argued that their clients' driving was simply not good enough for drive-by shootings.

KREVISZ: AUCKLAND'S (HALF)-SISTER CITY

Auckland City is not considered important enough to have full sister-city relations with any overseas cities. It does, however, have a 'half-sister city' in Krevisz, Uzbekistan's biggest city not under marshal law. Krevisz is a copper-mining town famous for its hospitality, especially to the many drug smugglers and gunrunners who use it as secure passage from Asia to Europe. Although Auckland has no cultural or historical ties to Uzbekistan, Krevisz was selected as a bilateral partner mainly because every other city was already spoken for, except Hamilton. It's not clear what benefits ordinary Jafas enjoy through having a half-sister city in Uzbekistan, but Auckland's mayor is invited to Krevisz once a year where he is ceremonially presented with 'two virgins of virtue good and true' and a mule.

IS AUCKLAND GAY?

Auckland is considered to be a liberal and gay-friendly city and has long been happy to embrace gay culture (in 1969 Auckland became the first city in New Zealand to admit openly gay animals to its zoo). Unfortunately, homosexuals tend not to feel so positive about Auckland, which is often regarded as something of a **gay lame duck**. However, there are a number of popular gay venues worth a visit, including SPQR (for food), Surrender Dorothy (for drink) and the bush in the middle of the Auckland Domain on Thursday nights (for casual get-togethers).

AUCKLAND'S MULLET PROBLEM

The Mullet, which is not indigenous to Auckland, is believed to have spread from unqualified hairdressers in Wellington's Hutt Valley. Experts traced the outbreak back to the early 1980s when poor people could only afford to have the sides and tops of their hair cut. A mutant strain of the style soon got loose and by 1997 it had spread to Auckland with the West of the city worst hit. By 2001 Jafas were demanding action. The Auckland City Council vowed to rid the city of this menace by the aerial spraying of West Auckland. However, these measures came too late. The epidemic was already out of control, having spread to South Auckland and many parts of the North Shore. Even the more fashionable parts of Auckland started to believe that the Mullet was 'in', such was the virulence of the style. It became clear that eradication was not an option and authorities could only hope to control the Mullet. In late 2002 MAF worked closely with international hair experts to reintroduce the **Mohawk** — this measure has so far proven very effective in bringing Mullet numbers under control. The council now monitors the Jafa Mullet population using a 'tag and release' programme.

MAF officers successfully trap a Mullet for tagging before releasing it back into the wild.

ESSENTIAL INFORMATION

POLICE

The Auckland Metropolitan Police Force is a highly visible presence within the city. Cops are recognisable by their smart blue uniforms and distinctive moustaches (this includes female officers). Auckland police are known for their restraint, except at riots, protests and any time they make an arrest. As a sign of non-aggression Jafa cops do not carry guns, only truncheons, grenades and, from 2005, Stinger ground-to-air missiles.

The official emergency number for the police is 111; however, because so many New Zealanders watch American police reality TV shows, 911 has been installed as a valid number (0900 GIRL COPS will also put you in touch with an 'officer').

THE AUCKLAND POLICE —
FROM KEYSTONE TO JUST KEY

The Auckland Metropolitan Police Force or **Pigs** as they are affectionately known is a well-trained body of men, women and dogs with a proud history. In 1918 the then Auckland Police Corps became the first force in the world to enlist women, homosexuals and priests. Only gay female parishioners were banned from joining.

Despite being expertly trained, Auckland police have long been hampered by a lack of funding. In 1998 a clerical error resulted in the force's much anticipated new uniforms being designed by Yves Saint Laurent. The resulting budget blowout meant less money for essential resources. Cutbacks resulted in the embarrassing sight of cops having to hitch-hike to the scene of a crime. Reported crime increased 26 per cent that year.

However, the police's new short-sleeved uniforms won 'Best Summer Collection' at the 1998 L'Oreal Fashion Awards. In 1999 public discontent with the police peaked when new research revealed that the average pizza delivery arrived 60 per cent faster than cops responding to an emergency call-out. The city council and government vowed to remedy the situation and the following year the police launched a pizza delivery arm. This failed to lower crime but the force's famous Hawaiian 5-0 became Auckland's best-selling pizza.

AUCKLAND'S WATER

Strict government recycling laws require that industrial waste must be recycled and this is why the effluent-rich Waikato River is now Auckland's water supply. The city had previously collected its drinking water from pristine catchment areas like the Hunua Ranges but since the building of the **Waikato River Pipeline** Aucklanders have been drinking Waikato River water, believed to be rich in nutrients and up to 23,000 trace chemicals. The heavily chlorinated end product is said to taste worse than pool water, which has caused big problems with thousands of Aucklanders now stealing school swimming pool water as a viable alternative.

The tapping of the Waikato River for Auckland's drinking water proved a huge success for the water supply industry — sales of bottled mineral water jumped 700 per cent.

NOISE CONTROL

Auckland City's famous Noise Control Corps enjoys broad-sweeping powers including the power to impound sound systems and the power to wear socks and sandals between the hours of 3 a.m. and 6 a.m. Because of excessive noise from suburban parties such as 21sts and wakes, Noise Control was recently granted the power to confiscate 'disagreeable' music including but not limited to, music louder than 80 decibels, music faster than 120 beats per minute and anything by Celine Dion. To make a complaint to Noise Control phone 0800 SHUT UP.

DRUGS IN AUCKLAND

Auckland has long had a serious drug problem. Quality drugs are still very hard to come by and are often grossly overpriced when compared to overseas centres. Many efforts have been made to improve the situation but the term 'Class A' is still no guarantee of quality.

THINGS AUCKLAND HAS THAT THE REST OF NEW ZEALAND DOESN'T (ACCORDING TO A SURVEY OF 1000 JAFAS)	THINGS THE REST OF NEW ZEALAND HAS THAT AUCKLAND DOESN'T (ACCORDING TO A SURVEY OF 1000 JAFAS)
Jobs	SARS
Electricity	Cholera
EFTPOS	Malaria
A gene pool	Typhoid
Judy Bailey	Dengue fever
A Ferrari dealership	Slavery
Conveniently hill-sized mountains	Sorcery
Big shiny planes that go overseas	Fiefdoms
Proper landmarks (i.e. structures big enough that jumping off them will kill you)	Moa
	Sounds that you can't hear even though they're called Sounds

AUCKLAND BY ITS MAJOR BOROUGHS

Auckland is made up of several cities or 'boroughs'. These are delineated along socio-economic boundaries. Generally, the closer to the city you get the greater the concentration of Jafas.

NORTH AUCKLAND

North Auckland takes its name from the fact that it is located to the north of the city, which many say is a good reflection of the level of imagination common in its residents.

NORTH AUCKLAND AT A GLANCE
POPULATION: Depends on traffic on the Harbour Bridge
LANGUAGE: English (excluding its vowels), Jafanese
MAIN INDUSTRY: Selling overpriced coastal property to rich foreigners and alcohol to under-age drinkers.

Placing the Jafa

The Mayor of North Auckland enjoys one of the area's legendary teenage parties.

CENTRAL AUCKLAND

Central Auckland is the spiritual home of Jafa culture. This ostensibly well-to-do precinct includes the central business district as well as the affluent central suburbs of Herne Bay, Ponsonby, Saint Mary's Bay and Grey Lynn. The area is popular with GUPPIES (Gay Urban Professionals), DINKs (Double Income No Kids) and MINIs (Massive Income No Idea).

CENTRAL AUCKLAND AT A GLANCE

POPULATION: A privileged few
LANGUAGE: English + French and Italian (when travelling or drunk at dinner parties)
MAIN INDUSTRY: Self-aggrandisement

EAST AUCKLAND

Many Jafas opposed to increased immigration point to East Auckland as an example of what can go wrong. Long-time East Auckland residents complain bitterly that the arrival of immigrants has transformed their reserved, sleepy, English-styled neighbourhood into a vibrant multicultural hub well worth a visit.

EAST AUCKLAND AT A GLANCE

POPULATION: Depends on current immigration policy
LANGUAGE: English, Pidgin English, Cantonese, Mandarin, Korean, Thai, Vietnamese, Japanese
MAIN INDUSTRY: Building large garish houses, subdividing according to feng shui principles

---

WEST AUCKLAND

A sprawling suburban backwater that spreads out to the Waitakere Ranges, West Auckland is often characterised as the home of bottle-blonde denim mini-wearing bimbos and panel-beating, boy-racing eejits who listen to thrash metal, smoke drugs and drive old Holdens. This is the stereotype; in fact, West Aucklanders drive a wide range of vehicles.

WEST AUCKLAND AT A GLANCE

POPULATION: Heaps, man
LANGUAGE: Slang
MAIN INDUSTRY: Panel beating, general beating

SOUTH AUCKLAND

In recent years South Auckland has received a lot of press, mainly crime stories, but any publicity is good publicity. The main selling point of South Auckland is that it is south enough of the city to be quiet but not so far south as to suffer the misfortune of actually being Hamilton.

SOUTH AUCKLAND AT A GLANCE

POPULATION: Lots and lots and lots
LANGUAGE: English, Maori, Nesian, Hip Hop
MAIN INDUSTRY: WINZ, manufacturing sports stars

---

4 ACTING THE JAFA
A GUIDE TO JAFA ETIQUETTE

Aucklanders have their own peculiar style of behaviour and way of communicating. Many visitors take the Jafa's aloofness and pronounced air of superiority to be **arrogance** and that's because it is. Nonetheless, a lot of misunderstanding exists about the character of Jafas. Those from outside Auckland often accuse Jafas of having no interest in them or their towns but it's not that Jafas have no interest, it's that they simply don't know about other places in New Zealand.

POLITICAL CORRECTNESS

Political correctness was an Auckland invention. While Mainlanders went about inventing revolutionary engines and machines to improve people's lives, it was left to Jafas to come up with a whole new philosophy on life. Like all great inventions, political correctness was born of necessity. It grew out of the liberal intelligentsia's collective guilt at feeling much smarter than most brown people and generally better off than the gay and disabled of Auckland. To relieve their guilt liberal Jafas decided to compensate minorities for their perceived disadvantages by inventing patronising euphemisms to describe them. An entire new lexicon was born and a suffocating culture of political correctness soon gripped Auckland. Political correctness continues to influence Jafa etiquette. Needless to say it is very important not to use racist or sexist language among Jafas, unless you are telling a joke in which case it is essential. Unsurprisingly, knowing exactly what is the right way to think can be a daunting prospect for the political-correctness-awareness-challenged. If you are uncertain, a good rule of thumb is to ask yourself: 'What would Judy Bailey do?'

DEALING WITH THE OPPOSITE SEX AS A JAFA

Auckland is a modern and contemporary city. Its **gender politics** are considered to be on the cutting edge of current thinking. New Zealand, after all, was the first country in the world to allow women the vote and although this was in fact merely a clerical error, it worked out favourably. In Auckland, as elsewhere in New Zealand, women fly planes, serve as police officers, sit on councils and even appear in swimsuit calendars. In short, Jafas acknowledge that women can do any job that men can do (except read maps and throw a ball properly). Most acts of chivalry are therefore considered outdated, unnecessary or just too expensive (e.g. buying a woman dinner at an Auckland restaurant). There are, however, a number of unspoken rules that govern how Jafa men and Jafa women should relate.

JAFA ETIQUETTE FOR MEN

- In some cities men walk on the side of the pavement nearest the road. Traditionally this was to prevent women from being splashed. Jafas observe this rule, too — men must not position themselves between women and shopfronts because this prevents Jafa women from checking their reflections in shop windows. This can be a problem area, as many Jafa men also like to check their reflections in shop windows. For this reason many Jafa couples walk in **single file**.

- When meeting a Jafa woman it is considered rude for a man to stare at her breasts, unless these are the subject of the conversation, e.g. 'They cost how much!?'
- Like many lending institutions, Jafa women often ask to see recent financial statements before agreeing to go out with a man. This is quite routine and men should not take offence. Furthermore, it is not uncommon for a Jafa woman to run a police check on a potential suitor before deciding whether this makes him more or less attractive.

JAFA ETIQUETTE FOR WOMEN

- It may be considered uncouth if you sleep with a Jafa man on the first date. Don't waste time sleeping; try to stay up all night having sex.
- At Jafa high-society gatherings it is considered backward if women don't show at least as much cleavage as the Wakatipu Basin.
- Never attempt to pass off fake breasts as 'natural' — if you get implants make sure they are unnaturally large in order to avoid this problem.
- A Jafa woman is not expected to have an opinion on the Auckland Blues, unless she is sleeping with one of them.

JAFA ETIQUETTE FAQS

Should I give up my seat for a Jafa woman on public transport?
It is not generally expected that a man should give up a seat for an able-bodied woman unless the woman is so incredibly able-bodied they would like an excuse to start a conversation with her.

Should I allow a man to open a door for me or is that allowing him to oppress me?
If a man opens a door for a woman in Auckland it is generally not seen as an act of oppression unless he actually removes it from its hinges and puts it on top of you.

Should I acknowledge people in the street?
You should acknowledge people in the street in as much as you make an effort not to run them down in your Land Rover. As for acknowledging pedestrians as you walk by, this is not generally done in Auckland. Jafas tend to keep to themselves and unsolicited greetings are left to prostitutes, drunks, perverts and Christians.

DRESS CODES

Auckland is a 'dress-up' city. The central city in particular calls for an unusually high standard of dress best described as 'smart-arse-casual'. The unspoken uniform of Jafas is black with a touch of black but more flamboyant Jafas sometimes add charcoal grey or even white.

BEACH DRESS

Nakedness on Auckland beaches is tolerated but this depends entirely on how beautiful the naked person is. Unfit or unpleasant-looking people who insist on going nude may cause offence. Discretion is advised. If you consider yourself to be in this category, it may pay to compensate by having an attractive friend accompany you.

JAFA PHONE ETIQUETTE

Cellphones are commonplace nowadays but Jafas were the first Kiwis to embrace mobiles when they first appeared in the late 1980s. The fact that early models were the size of fax machines did not stop Jafas from recognising the cellphone's potential for enhancing the user's self-importance. Suddenly Aucklanders had an excuse to talk loudly about themselves in public places. The cellphone quickly became an important means of self-expression in Jafa culture.

WHAT TO LOOK FOR IN A JAFA CELLPHONE

In Auckland you will most likely be judged by your cellphone and how you use it rather than by your car. As a rough guide, your cellphone should be small enough to present a choking hazard and yet be able to register on the Richter Scale when set to vibrate mode.

Acting the Jafa

This Jafa male demonstrates textbook cellphone technique.
Within 10 paces surrounding onlookers already know he not only works in
advertising but that he is in the middle of a very big campaign.

USING YOUR CELLPHONE TO GET OUT OF A BORING CONVERSATiON

If you are trapped in a boring conversation with a Jafa (which happens often), effective use of your cellphone can help you abort without appearing rude. Today's vibrating cellphones mean you can answer a call without anyone else being aware your phone has rung. Wait until the Jafa you are talking to is in the midst of a long rant, then suddenly reach into your pocket, produce your phone and pretend to answer it. Express interest in the imaginary call and then point out to the other person that the call is from London and you have to take it. Walk away briskly.

CELLPHONE USE IN CARS

Cellphone use while driving is acceptable and indeed encouraged in Auckland. However, care should be taken to ensure road hazards and driving concerns don't distract you from an important call.

BASIC JAFA CELLPHONE ETIQUETTE FOR THE NON-USER

It is considered rude to interrupt a Jafa while he or she is using a cellphone. Exceptions to this rule include:

If the cellphone actually belongs to you;

If the cellphone is so old and large it is causing embarrassment;

If you are warning the Jafa they are about to be hit by a bus;

If you are warning the bus driver they are about to be hit by a Jafa.

MISCELLANEOUS JAFA ETIQUETTE

VISITING

It is considered rude to offer to do the dishes after a meal as this is deemed to be implying your guests don't have the latest dishwasher — an offensive inference in Jafa culture. It is considered polite to compliment Jafas on their homes and furnishings. A good way to ingratiate oneself with a Jafa is to ask how much everything in their house cost and then nod approvingly, regardless of the answers.

TIPPING

Tipping is not really expected in Auckland restaurants unless the waiter or waitress does something exceptional such as smile or bring you the right meal.

CONVERSING

Very few topics are taboo among Jafas but there are still limits to what is considered polite conversation in Auckland. The following topics are not generally discussed in Jafa circles:

The rest of New Zealand.

SWEARING

As a relatively civilised lot, Jafas tend to take a dim view of swearing. The use of expletives and coarse language of any kind is generally unacceptable among Jafas, unless you are talking about: Australians; Asians; Indians; Persians; immigrants in general; refugees; beneficiaries; overstayers; vegetarians; vegans; Mormons, Hari Krishnas, gays; straights; Hamilton; Christchurch; Wellington; Wellington's weather; the southern motorway, traffic; crossing the harbour bridge; motorists; pedestrians; John Banks; Helen Clark; Maori; the Treaty; the Rugby World Cup (any year except 1987); the weather; Brad Butterworth; Russell Coutts; Russell Crowe; Russell township; the economy; the woman off the Briscoes ads; taxis; taxi drivers; the public transport system or lack of; the health system or lack of; dog owners; dog attacks; private school fees; parking wardens; tow-truck drivers; the cost of a muffin at Auckland International Airport; Helen Clark again; students; the Canterbury Crusaders; drugs; drug users and the P-epidemic.

ORDERING COFFEE

In reality all coffee tastes the same (coffee-flavoured); nonetheless just ordering a coffee in Auckland can be a challenge for the uninitiated. If you are unsure, you can make things easier simply by randomly combining any of the following words in any order and then asking for a cup:

mocha	frappa	cappu	chai	soy
long	short	black	white	double
single	lite	decaf	recaf	Gidday Cath

HOW TO PLAY COFFEE BINGO

Enter any Ponsonby Road café with a pen and paper and take a seat near the counter. Write down the names of coffees as you hear them ordered. When you have a full column like the one above, yell 'Bingo' and receive the coffee of your choice.

TOUCHING THE JAFA

Handling the Jafa is a skill that must be acquired by anyone who hopes to advance socially or professionally in Auckland. Touching is not something well understood by most Jafas and they are not renowned for being the most 'touchy-feely' Kiwis. There is usually little physical contact between casually acquainted Jafas outside of rugby (playing or watching). More intimate touching is generally reserved for partners or working professionals. In most parts of New Zealand the **handshake** is the most commonly accepted means of handling another person and Auckland is no different. In fact, in some mature Jafa marriages this is the only form of contact. It is therefore important to know how to **give good hand**. Be sure to make eye contact when shaking hands with a Jafa but KEEP IT BRIEF. Anything longer than a few seconds could be regarded as staring or worse, friendliness. Remember that hand shaking is exactly like sex, it should:

- Be firm but painless;
- Involve eye contact;
- Take only two or three pumps;
- Last about three seconds.

COMPLIMENTARY JAFA BOOKMARK

5 LOVING
THE JAFA
DATING AND DIVORCE

'Dating' and 'divorce' describe the two periods of any Jafa's life when the most momentous events occur. The section in between is called 'marriage'. In Auckland this is a strictly transitional stage.

DATING — FIRST BRAVE STEPS TOWARDS MARRIAGE AND INEVITABLE DIVORCE

Dating Jafas can be a confusing process. The traditional boundaries of Kiwi society do not apply in Auckland. Jafa men are often more in touch with their feminine side than Jafa women, who are often more ambitious than men, who often dress better than the women. Anyone hoping to date a Jafa must come to terms with this, or alternatively, date only foreigners.

JAFA MEN TODAY

Auckland is not considered a good place to meet men. A severe shortage of quality eligible males is the biggest problem. A common complaint is that 'all the good men are gay'. In fact, according to a recent survey of Jafa women, as many as 85 per cent of Auckland men are gay, and of the remaining 15 per cent, 90 per cent are either married or dead.

A typical metrosexual Jafa.

Any female hoping to court Jafa men will need to become familiar with the city's indigenously urban breed of men, sometimes referred to as the **metrosexual**. In Auckland, a metrosexual is defined as a mildly heterosexual urbanite who is easily aroused by pictures of both men *and* women in the pages of *Metro* magazine.

Jen the Jafa says:
'The only history that's important to me is credit history. No credit history and they're history.'

JAFA WOMEN TODAY

Auckland is not considered a good place to meet women. Despite the ready availability of single females, actually meeting them is difficult. A recently released UNESCO report found that Auckland had the lowest incidence of casual sex amongst OECD countries. It is widely acknowledged as the **Southern Hemisphere's most difficult city in which to get laid**.

WHAT DO JAFA WOMEN ACTUALLY WANT?

The answer to this question is so utterly simple it is often overlooked. What Jafa women look for in a man is **money**. While they also look for other qualities (such as intelligence, sensitivity and the ability to hang a wet towel off his manhood) these prerogatives are easily overridden by cash.

QUALITIES JAFA WOMEN SAY THEY VALUE	TRANSLATION
Intelligence	Intelligence about how to make money
Sensitivity	Sensitivity to my financial needs
Credibility	Credit-rating-ability
A sense of humour	A sense of humour about how much of his money I like to spend
A good job	A good job being one in which his income tax exceeds my whole salary
Height	Height, bearing in mind that each million a man possesses adds a foot to his 'effective height'

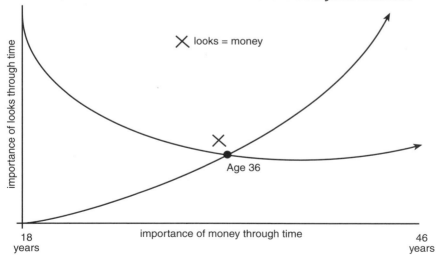

IMPORTANCE OF LOOKS VERSUS MONEY FOR JAFA FEMALE

HOW TO MEET A JAFA

Jafas meet in a variety of ways — at the beach, at work, in divorce court. Up to 30 per cent of Asian Jafa newly-weds met their partner at the scene of a car accident*. But these kinds of meetings occur by chance. Where do you go if you are deliberately trying to meet someone in Auckland?

HOW TO GO ABOUT DELIBERATELY TRYING TO MEET SOMEONE IN AUCKLAND

The key to deliberately trying to meet someone in Auckland is to look as though you are not deliberately trying to meet someone. A good way to do this is to go to any place where there are lots of people deliberately trying to meet someone. If there are lots of people deliberately trying to meet someone, the fact that you are deliberately trying to meet someone may be less obvious, thus increasing your chances of deliberately meeting someone. Or just meeting someone by accident.

PLACES FOR DELIBERATELY TRYING TO MEET SOMEONE

Auckland does not have any official singles bars like those that are popular in overseas cities but it does have **meat markets** — the Jafa equivalent. These popular establishments are called 'meat markets' because they are associated with women referred to as 'mutton dressed as lamb' as well as young women known as 'lambs to the slaughter'. They may also be frequented by middle-aged men known as 'meatheads'. While meat markets are popular with those keen to test New Zealand's age-of-consent legislation, they are not the first choice of Jafas serious about finding a long-term partner.

ALTERNATIVE WAYS TO MEET SINGLE JAFAS

INTERNET DATING

One advantage of Internet dating is that it provides a way of dating for those Jafas too shy to meet people face to face. One disadvantage is that you only find people who are too shy to meet people face to face. But perhaps the biggest problem of Internet dating is people using the anonymity of computers to misrepresent themselves. This

Jeff the Jafa says:
'I've met some really special women through Internet dating. I still keep seeing some of them. Mostly in court.'

* This is known as 'meeting someone by accident'.

problem was all too well highlighted when, in 2003, a dating chat-room bungle resulted in Yasser Arafat meeting Ariel Sharon for coffee at a hip Jerusalem café. Newcomers tend to think that around half the people on Internet dating sites are sad, pathetic, social retards but this is not so. In reality, the ratio is closer to three-quarters.

WARNING! When dating on the Internet it is important to exercise caution. Geeks hunting for unsuspecting young women have been known to masquerade as normal people on Internet dating web sites. Geeks and nerds often attempt to entice normal women with the promise of romantic dinners and walks on the beach. Once contact has been made the women are usually lured into hotel rooms where they are exposed to appalling personal hygiene, made to dress up in indecent clothing and forced to play games of Dungeons and Dragons they did not consent to. If you detect any kind of suspicious behaviour, such as attempts to discuss *Star Trek* or *Star Wars*, report this immediately to the police.

Jen the Jafa says:
'I had no idea there were so many single guys on the Net. This one guy, Wolverine_654, was a real charmer. He was suave, sexy and really knew how to make a lady feel like a lady. So we met for a drink. To this day he is the most eloquent 10-year-old I have ever met.'

JURY DUTY

With Auckland's high rate of crime, jury duty is an excellent opportunity to meet a potential Jafa mate. The intensive closeting of 12 people over sometimes extended periods (often in a hotel) provides an excellent opportunity to get to know new people and explore whatever possibilities may arise, even as you decide the fate of an alleged criminal. It also gives you access to a range of attractive lawyers, who are highly sought-after Jafa partners (both professionally and romantically).

LOVE ON THE JURY: JANIE'S STORY

'I met Bruce on a double-murder trial. Our love was forged during 12 hours of deliberation over whether the accused had intended to kill her husband and his lover when she ran them down in her Pajero, then repeatedly beat them with the grinder attachment from a $5000 espresso coffee maker. I was impressed by how passionately Bruce argued that the prosecution's case failed to show premeditated intent. It was a side of him I don't think I would have seen had we met in a bar or nightclub. Anyway, the accused was convicted of murder and sentenced to 17 years, which is exactly how long Bruce and I intend to be married.'

THE SUPERMARKET

The supermarket is an increasingly popular place to meet eligible Jafas. In Auckland there are codes for identifying oneself as being single and on the prowl while food shopping. These were co-opted from the gay community, which has been communicating in code for years. In the supermarket the possession and positioning of **produce** is used to signal a prospecting Jafa's status and preferences. Below is a basic guide.

Banana between two melons
— Man seeks woman

Banana between four melons
— Man seeks two women

Shrivelled corn next to melon
— Married man seeks extra-
curricular activity

Two bananas side by side
— Man seeks man

Banana next to leg of lamb
— Man seeks animal

Melon next to banana
— Woman seeks man

Loving the Jafa

Melon next to bunch of bananas — woman seeks as many men as possible

Melon next to melon — Woman seeks woman

Melon next to marrow — Woman seeks especially well-endowed man

Lemons — Not available

Melon, banana, apple, orange and lemon — Planning a fruit salad

GOING ON A DATE

WHAT IS A DATE IN AUCKLAND?

A date is two people meeting at a certain time and place to mutually enjoy a given activity. It may involve the exchange of small gifts but is usually designed to culminate in the exchange of bodily fluids.

ASKING FOR A DATE

There are many ways of asking for a date but most Jafas prefer not to operate face to face. Using some written form of invitation is preferred. In this electronic age of speedy communications, writing via text message or email is a good way to ask for a date. This is favoured among those Jafas too busy or too pretentious to talk directly. Writing also allows you to set the tone of your invitation without fear of stuttering, tripping over your words or accidentally saying 'fuck'. There are good and bad written invitations. Compare the examples below.

GOOD INVITATION

Dearest Jenny,

I hope this letter finds you well. Would you like to meet for coffee? I'm free around 5.30 p.m. Saturday. It would be great if you could make it then because, if we sit outside, I'll be able to watch the rays of the setting sun catch the natural highlights of your luxuriant strawberry-blonde hair.

Love,

Jeff

BAD INVITATION

Hey Jenny,

Wanna have sex? I'm free around 5.30 Saturday, which means you should be able to get away by about 25 to six.

Cheers,

Jeff

P.S. Wear something tight and a gas mask.

DATE TO IMPRESS

Once your invitation has been accepted it's time to plan the date. Remember that the activities you choose should not simply be fun and entertaining, they should be designed to impress your date.

TECHNIQUES FOR IMPRESSING A JAFA FEMALE ON A DATE

USE A BUSINESS CARD

Have a business card printed for your date. The card should list your date's name. Be sure to observe the correct spelling. Explain that where you're taking her there are going to be a lot of paparazzi. Many of them will want to photograph you and they will all want to know who she is. Point out that the card will save time as well as increasing the chances of her photo appearing correctly captioned in the society pages of *Metro* magazine.

USE A PORSCHE

Jafa women love sports cars. The leather seats feel good against their highly aerobicised, sunbed-enhanced legs. Also, expensive European sports cars suggest a high level of fiscal liquidity in the Jafa male. But maybe you don't have a 911. A good alternative is to 'fake the Porsche'.

Loving the Jafa

Have your date meet you at a café or bar in an area with a high density of Porsches. When she arrives lead her to the nearest parked Porsche. Be sure to choose a late-model Porsche. Never choose a Porsche 924 (these are considered the poor man's Porsche). As you sidle up to the car, produce a genuine Porsche key ring (you can buy these from any car accessories shop). Approach the car in a roundabout way, lingering by the driver's door but being careful not to touch the car. Take a moment to point out what a happy coincidence it is that the car's colour matches her eyes. Just as you are about to click the auto-lock on your key ring suddenly stop. Explain you have just remembered that you will be drinking tonight. Immediately hail a cab and leave before the car's owner emerges.

STOP AT A HOUSE AUCTION

On the way to the restaurant explain to your date that you have to stop at a house auction. Choose a very expensive house in a very nice part of Auckland. Tell her that spending time with her is so important you couldn't postpone your date just because you're making a million-dollar investment tonight. At the auction be the first to bid. Offer to let her bid on your behalf. This involves her and makes her feel like you are already a couple. This will also indulge her latent nesting instincts. Be careful to keep track of the auction or you may end up actually buying the house. Just when the bidding starts to get serious pretend to be fatally distracted by your date's outfit. Pretend to fall into a trance but snap out of this when you hear the auctioneer's hammer fall. Explain that you're not disappointed you missed out on the house because after seeing her in it you've realised it's not the right home for the two of you. Proceed immediately to the restaurant.

THE DUCK TECHNIQUE

A good place for a romantic afternoon date is the Auckland Domain. It's leafy, serene and has a duck pond. Ducks present a good opportunity for you to showcase your caring side to the Jafa female. You can do this by poisoning a duck. Take your date on a stroll by the pond. Make a point of identifying by name the different species of duck (this may require some prior research). Point out how sad it is that some ducks are endangered. Now see your date to a park bench and excuse yourself to 'use the toilet'.

The Duck Technique Step 1 — apprehend a duck.

Once out of sight, apprehend a duck (the larger the duck the better). Be careful to muffle its panicked quacking. Take about half a pellet of rat poison and introduce this to the duck. Wait for the duck to become drowsy then deposit it under a nearby tree, being careful to note the precise location of the tree. Return to your date, point out that it's getting late. Lead your date towards the tree where you left the poisoned duck. Hold her hand as you walk towards the tree. MAKE SURE YOU SPOT THE DUCK BEFORE SHE DOES. Break off and run to investigate. Explain that the duck is obviously distressed. Take the duck in your hands. Tell your date you have seen these symptoms in ducks before, when you were in Laos, so you know that the duck needs immediate medical attention. Drive the duck to the nearest bird sanctuary. Phone ahead on your cellphone and give a description of the duck's symptoms as well as an estimate of its age, weight and sex. The Jafa female should be impressed by your applicable general knowledge of aviary ailments. Once you have safely delivered the duck, comment on how all this has made you hungry. Suggest a meal. Take your date straight to a restaurant (be sure there is no duck on the menu).

DATING AT SPEED

Speed dating has enjoyed some popularity in Auckland, where time-poor Jafas have embraced the opportunity of dating up to 10 people in one night. However, in some parts of the city, speed dating has already been superseded by **drive-by dating**. On a drive-by date a single Jafa man drives past the home of a single Jafa woman, catching a glimpse of her as she stares out the window of her front room. The Jafa woman is able to appraise her potential mate by the make and condition of his car. If the first date goes well a second date begins immediately with the man performing a U-turn at the end of the street and driving past again. This time the Jafa woman exposes more of herself from the window. The advantage of drive-by dating is that participants don't have to leave their cars or homes and there's no obligation. After two or three drive-bys the woman may agree to be picked up and driven around the block to see if there's any chemistry.

Loving the Jafa

TIP LIKE A JAFA

When it comes to the tip, surprise your date by asking the waiter for his bank account number. Produce your PDA cellphone with mobile Internet. Explain that you are transferring a sizeable tip from an offshore account into his personal account by direct credit. Point out that with the way the exchange rate is at the moment it's really going to increase his 'net'. Explain that you will have the bank slug the transaction 'The service was excellent'.

THE RING TECHNIQUE

Male infidelity among Jafas is easily explained. When a Jafa man is single a Jafa female senses this using her Jafa woman's intuition (her girlfriend told her). This triggers a gland in the Jafa female's brain known as the **proprietary gland**, which controls the amount of interest a woman can show in a man. When a woman learns that a man is available the proprietary gland shuts down completely, contracting and causing the onset of a headache and a pronounced disinterest in the single man. This is often accompanied by a heavy malaise and may result in the desire to draw a hot bath and read *Cosmo*. Conversely, when a woman detects that a man is married, the proprietary gland is stimulated; it swells up to six times its normal size and begins to resemble a baboon's posterior (though on a much smaller scale). The Jafa female suddenly experiences an uncontrollable attraction to the unavailable man. This is why married men often complain of having to beat women off and quite often, having been overwhelmed, give up beating them off and start sleeping with them. Meanwhile, the single Jafa man languishes in a lonely no-man's land of uncertainty, completely unaware that a gland the size of a raisin is running his social life.

But Jafa men have developed their own way of giving nature's complex play of psychological triggers a helping hand — it's called the **Ring Technique** or 'wearing a gold wedding band'. Some men have for years used this ploy to trick women into liking them. Jafa women should be wary of men using the Ring Technique to suggest they are married. Always ask to see a man's wife before deciding to find him attractive.

HOW TO ENDURE A DULL DATE — USING BEER GOGGLES

If your Jafa date is not progressing well and you do not appear to be having a good time you may elect to don **beer goggles**. Beer goggles are based on the more traditional 'rose-tinted glasses', which have long been used to improve the way people feel about things. Beer goggles, if used properly, can transform even the most mind-numbingly dull evening into an enjoyable and eventful night out. Beer goggles must be applied gradually in order to be effective. This is achieved by drinking beer steadily but excessively within a limited time frame (alternatively drink chardonnay in order to apply chardonnay goggles). If applied correctly things start to look better within a couple of hours because beer goggles enhance your ability to appreciate even the limited charms of a dull date. After four or more hours the date should have become the best thing that's ever happened to you. You may even see your date as someone you could spend the rest of your night with. Exercise caution when using beer goggles as they sometimes work on friends of the same sex, causing the user to profess undying love to old school chums. Once beer goggles have been applied they cannot be easily removed and may affect your judgement and your standards for up to eight hours. Also, remember that beer goggles are effective only at night and will not improve your view of things in the cold light of day.

HOW TO DATE THE JAFA MALE — THE IMPORTANCE OF PLAYING HARD TO GET

All Jafa women must learn how to play hard to get. Playing hard to get adds a premium to the Jafa female in the eyes of the Jafa male by making her seem like more of a challenge. If properly executed, playing hard to get can make a woman seem unobtainable and therefore **respectable**. This in turn makes her **desirable**. In Auckland, being seen as respectable and desirable is more respectable and desirable than actually getting together with a man and running the risk of appearing **easy**. This is why Jafa women always play hard to get. In order to be effective, the discipline of playing hard to get must be RIGIDLY ADHERED TO, even if this behaviour seems harsh.

BASIC PLAYING HARD TO GET — IGNORING MEN

This is the essential skill that all Jafa women must master. Only by completely ignoring men can a Jafa woman maintain that sense of **mystery** and **enigma** that is essential to her being attractive. Observe mature Jafa women in bars — they are masters of the art of paying men no attention whatsoever. This is why Auckland's bars are full of people standing around ignoring each other. Few achieve their aim of meeting someone but there is a tremendous sense of mystery.

When playing hard to get NEVER:
- Look at a man;
- Talk to a man;
- Open your mouth;
- Respond directly to a man who speaks to you;
- Use any kind of body language.

PLAYING HARD TO GET WHEN DATING

If you have followed the basic rules of playing hard to get you may, somehow, have been asked on a date. Many novice Jafa women make the mistake of thinking this is the time to start easing off. In fact, this is the time to redouble your efforts. You should not only be playing hard to get while dating, you should be playing *harder* to get as time wears on. This way you compensate for the fact that you appear easier to get the more time you spend with your date. This kind of advanced playing hard to get involves the sometimes challenging skill of proactively and aggressively ignoring your date.

HOW TO PLAY HARD TO GET ON A DINNER DATE

- Do not speak.
- Do not eat.
- DO NOT look at your date directly.
- Wink at the waiter.
- Drink only water (indifferently).
- Make a long phone call to a mystery man during the main course.
- Openly fellate the waiter.

A lot of you may be thinking, 'This is surely playing *too* hard to get — a phone call during the main course? That's going too far.' This may well seem extreme, even unnatural, but this kind of pronounced evasive behaviour is the only way to make the congenitally apathetic Jafa male take interest. If any relationship were to form, the playing hard to get philosophy should still be observed, in order to keep your Jafa male on his toes and totally attentive.

HOW TO PLAY HARD TO GET DURING SEX

- Leave your pantyhose on;
- Assume the 'Starfish' position and don't move;

- Maintain an expression that suggests you are trying to remember your fourth-form geography teacher's first name;
- Do not yawn (this may appear erotic);
- Frequently change channels.

HOW TO PLAY HARD TO GET WHILST IN A RELATIONSHIP

- Ignore all phone calls and messages;
- Wear dark glasses and fake moustaches;
- Disavow all knowledge of your previous life;
- Move to Iran.

If you follow these guidelines, we guarantee the Jafa male will always be utterly fascinated by you.

Jen the Jafa says:
'My grandmother always taught me to play hard to get with men. She's a fine example. After 57 years she finally found the man of her dreams. Admittedly, the man of her dreams was by then any man without a catheter bag but she's deliriously happy now, even accounting for the dementia.'

STRATEGICALLY DROPPING YOUR STANDARDS

If you have played your cards right, you should have been able to palm off the advances of all Jafa men, thus enhancing your mystery and enigma and making you highly desirable to any male who has succeeded in actually noticing you. By now you should be in your mid-30s and approaching your sexual peak. This is the time to consider dropping your standards drastically in order to get a boyfriend before it's too late. All Jafa women know when it is time to begin dropping their standards because of an in-built time-keeping facility known as the **biological clock**. The biological clock is like a real alarm clock in that it can be set to 'snooze'. However, many women make the mistake of ignoring their biological clock until it is nearly too late. Around age 36 it suddenly overwhelms them. The Jafa woman panics and marries an insurance salesman or some similarly soft option. To avoid disappointment, consider lowering your standards earlier and do so gradually as you become more desperate.

FURTHER DOWN THE TRACK

How do you know when you have moved on from dating to having a fully fledged Jafa relationship? Well, there are a number of indicators, which, seeing as they are indicators, indicate that you are in a serious relationship. Learn to look for the telltale signs. You may be in a serious relationship if:

- You have a nickname for each other;
- You have a nickname for each other's sexual organs;
- You have children;
- You hate each other.

If any of the above indicators are present you may feel you are ready to take the plunge and get married — and therefore divorced.

DIVORCE

Astute readers will notice that a chapter on marriage is absent from this book. This is because a lot has already been written about marriage. Not nearly as much has been written about divorce, even though many people spend more time divorced than they do married. In most cultures divorce is regarded as some kind of critical failure in the nuclear family. In some countries women who want a divorce are stoned to death. In Auckland, when a woman asks for a divorce it's considered a shrewd career move. Divorce is a badge of honour among Jafas. It signifies the completion of a domestic tour of duty. In fact, according to the *Way of the Jafa*, you're not ready for marriage until you've been through a divorce.

Jeff the Jafa says:
'It's all fun and games until someone loses a house.'

PLANNING YOUR DIVORCE

Many couples spend a great deal of time planning their wedding. Statistics prove that most Jafa brides spend more time deliberating over their choice of wedding dress than they do over their choice of husband. But how many couples plan ahead for their divorce? A divorce quite often has a much bigger effect on a person's life than their marriage and yet many couples act like it's never going to happen. Statistics say otherwise; that's why smart Jafas prepare for their divorce even before their marriage.

WHEN TO DIVORCE

Any time of year is a fine time for divorce in Auckland, except over the December/ January holiday period when lawyers are vacationing and the courts are closed.

HOW TO PROPOSE DIVORCE

Some people go to extraordinary lengths with their marriage proposals, even though they already know the answer when they pop the question. A proposal for divorce is far more crucial because once you have decided to divorce, all your future plans depend on getting your spouse to agree. There is no right way or wrong way to propose a divorce, although as a general rule men should not go down on one knee as this leaves them vulnerable to attack. Ideally, Jafas try to find a way that clearly calls for a divorce but is still fun to do. The following is a list of suggestions.

GOOD WAYS TO PROPOSE DIVORCE

- Sleep with another person;
- Sleep with several other persons;
- Suggest your spouse sleeps with another person;
- Suggest your spouse sleeps with several other persons and provide them a list of names and numbers;
- Refuse to sleep with your spouse without a lawyer present;
- Sleep with your lawyer while your spouse is present.

THE DISENGAGEMENT NOTICE

In Auckland, when a divorce has been agreed between a couple, it is traditional for the couple to announce the happy news by posting a **Disengagement Notice** in a daily newspaper. These usually look like the one in the example below.

Loving the Jafa

Bourneworth, Shaft & Smythe Barristers are pleased to announce the disengagement and pending divorce proceedings of their client Jane Mills.

The disengagement notice is usually followed some time later by the **official divorce notice**, which usually looks like the one in the example below.

Bourneworth, Shaft, Smythe and Mills are pleased to announce the successful divorce and settlement of their client Jane Mills.

HOLDING A DISENGAGEMENT PARTY

Weddings involve the showering of the lucky couple with gifts, many of them domestic appliances and other useful implements. However, it's when they divorce that Jafas are more likely to need a toaster and a microwave, having lost these small but important things in the settlement. Holding a disengagement party ahead of the divorce is a great way to re-equip for Auckland life at the expense of your friends.

According to Jafa etiquette, a disengagement party is traditionally hosted by the divorcing party's lawyer. Being a happy social occasion, a divorce reception is also an excellent opportunity to 'get back on the horse' by sizing up potential new partners.

WHAT TO WEAR TO A DIVORCE

Marriage is all about looking great and divorce should be no different. Pick out some outfits that will make you look a million dollars in court or at least the several hundred thousand dollars you intend to walk away with. Make sure you purchase these outfits while you and your partner's joint account is still open. It makes wearing them all the more satisfying when your jilted spouse knows that they were purchased with money meant for your anniversary trip to Fiji.

ENJOYING YOUR NEWFOUND FREEDOM

The key to a happy divorce is putting some real distance between you and your ex-spouse, not just emotionally but physically. You can do this by taking what Jafas call a **moneymoon**. A moneymoon is the holiday taken immediately after a divorce using the money from the divorce settlement. This is a popular trend among female Jafas, who tend to fare best in divorce settlements, but is also the preferred choice of male Jafas, who see a moneymoon as an opportunity to display disposable income in order to attract a new, much younger mate. Female moneymoons are usually taken in European cities like Paris or Rome where eligible bachelors are found. Male moneymoons are often taken in Asian cities such as Bangkok where the favourable exchange rate enhances the Jafa male's appearance of sound liquidity.

WHAT ABOUT THE CHILDREN?

It's important to consider the fate of your children in any divorce. To avoid them feeling left out, involve your kids by using them to emotionally blackmail your spouse. Using your children as collateral in a divorce makes the children feel valued and loved. It's also important that your children do not fall into the trap of blaming themselves for the marriage breakdown. Avoid this by sitting your children down and explaining what an arsehole/ bitch your spouse is and how you wish you'd never married him/her.

It's important that your children don't come away thinking divorce is a bad thing. Equally, there's no reason why divorcees should regret their divorces. A properly planned and executed divorce can be rewarding and fufilling, both spiritually and financially.

6 HOUSING THE JAFA
BUYING A HOME IN AUCKLAND

Relatively speaking, houses are the most expensive things that can be bought in Auckland (excluding electric-toothbrush heads and office stationery). You practically have to take out a mortgage to buy a house in Auckland. Nonetheless, owning one's own home is central to the *Way of the Jafa*.

PROBLEMS WITH BUYING IN AUCKLAND

The biggest problem with buying property in Auckland is that all the houses are f**king expensive. That's it. Nothing can be said that will make any difference to that.

Auckland's property market has enjoyed a tremendous boom over the last 10 years. In December 2003 a buyer paid $564,000 for this sign in Herne Bay. Its previous owner had paid just $190,000 for it a year earlier.

WHEN TO BUY

When it comes to timing your purchase the first thing to admit is that you're already far too late. The time to buy was when you could pick up most of the waterfront with the extra blankets from your spare room and that jar of buttons in the shed. Times have changed. Those early Maori guardians of the land have long gone, replaced by a much more savage tribe of people who, like them, live off the land — by selling it and taking a big cut.

REAL ESTATE AGENTS

Despite what the name suggests, 'real estate agents' are not a more authentic incarnation of some earlier breed of 'estate agents'. Furthermore, they are not 'agents' in the true sense of the word, like 'CIA agents' (although they do sit around in cars outside houses for extended periods).

WHAT TO LOOK FOR IN A REAL ESTATE AGENT

The number one quality you want your Jafa real estate agent to have is honesty. They should also have houses to show you — that helps. Unfortunately, honesty is a quality very difficult to gauge in strangers, particularly Jafas. Make sure the agent is a member of the Real Estate Institute of New Zealand, as opposed to, say, the Highway 61 motorcycle gang or the New Zealand First Party.

There are two fundamental truths about real estate agents that prospective Jafa homebuyers should be aware of:

1. They do absolutely nothing.
2. They are terrified people will realise they do absolutely nothing.

Real estate agents will try to distract the novice Jafa homebuyer from the fact that they do absolutely nothing by talking endlessly about 'the market' in terms that imply the market is a close personal friend of theirs. They will make advanced, complex and highly technical statements such as the following:

- 'The market is good.'
- 'The market is up.'
- 'The market is firm.'
- 'Look out! The market's behind you!'

WHAT FACTORS INFLUENCE THE MARKET?

No one knows for sure what makes Auckland house prices suddenly increase. Many attribute the boom of 2003 to such factors as *The Lord of The Rings* trilogy (but this really only affected property prices in Mordor and parts of the Shire). In Auckland the market is mainly determined by the number of people selling their baches, boathouses or dog kennels on the coast for utterly fantastic sums in order to pay for villas in Central Auckland that cost only slightly less than an F-18 Fighter Jet. If this number is high the market is 'strong'. If this number is low the market is merely 'booming'. The market is also influenced by the number of DIY home make-over shows on TV. At the time of writing there were 37 Auckland-made DIY home make-over shows on television and as a result the market was 'stable'.

OTHER FACTORS THAT INFLUENCE THE AUCKLAND PROPERTY MARKET:

Rachel Hunter's career;
Rachel Hunter's choice of boyfriend;
How well we lose at the Rugby World Cup;
How well Judy Bailey is ageing.

Auckland's property market has a long history of growth, as this 1843 story from the *New Zealand Herald* shows.

AUCKLAND PROPERTY BOOM CAUSE OF MUCH AROUSAL

Last month, being February, the price of 10,000 hectares of bushland breached the 100 blankets' price limit for the first time, causing real estate experts to predict with surety it may yet exceed 200 blankets or 20 muskets per 1000 hectares by the middle of the year. The increase in sales has been attributed to both increasing numbers of courageous pioneers from the Motherland and the amazing generosity of the natives who have demonstrated an admirable willingness to learn the time-honoured concept of individual ownership as the right of all God-fearing men. 'The spirit of goodwill and trust that informs each new sale is a tribute to the right-thinking fairness of Britain's settlers and to the dignity of the Maori race,' declared Mr George Davies, President of the Auckland Settlers' Land Confiscation Association. When asked to explain the healthy boom in land acquisitions Mr Davies did not dally in citing the high level of demand for arable land worthy of development and the Maori's apparent fascination for shiny buttons and the like. 'Clearly the savages are fast learning the concept of a market, such that they may profit handsomely from their land sales with all manner of wondrous weapons and woven fabrics of the utmost calibre, the likes of which they, in their noble but primitive existence, have never seen.' Another contributing factor was said to be the natives' entirely novel concept of what land is and should be, this having encouraged them to be most suitably and agreeably generous in their dealings, thus enhancing land sales throughout the colony. Buyers have continued to make all due haste in acquiring what land they can from the natives. 'The success of Britain's mighty settlers in working so faithfully with the natives will no doubt stand this young nation of ours in good stead,' said Mr Davies, a leading Freemason and Protestant.

UNDERSTANDING THE LISTINGS — A GUIDE TO REAL ESTATE ADVERTISING COPY

'First time on the market in X years'	Vendor has died. Check to be sure he/she didn't die in the house; it may be haunted
'Includes prominent water feature'	Leaks like a sieve
'Great for entertaining'	The house is actually an adult cinema
'Breath-taking décor'	The last owner painted all the walls so thickly that the fumes are still a problem
'The ultimate do-up'	You could 'do up' to half a million dollars worth of damage to your finances, just in making it liveable
'Split level'	The floor between the dining and living rooms has collapsed, creating a step
'Peaceful surrounds'	Borders a cemetery
'Rustic'	Fire-damaged
'Buyers must inspect'	It's possible there are body parts hidden in the walls
'Good indoor/outdoor flow'	Susceptible to flooding
'Realistic vendor will sell'	Vendor has a sizeable debt with the local Headhunters gang. This could be an issue if the Headhunters, seeking reprisals, burn down your house with you in it

WHAT KIND OF DWELLING?

The Jafa homebuyer must consider many different options when buying a home. Each homebuyer must ask themselves a number of questions that are pertinent to them. For instance, does the dwelling have the necessary space for: kids, horses, a P-lab?

COMMON TYPES OF JAFA DWELLINGS

THE VILLA

This is probably the most sought-after dwelling among Jafas. Villas are prized for their draughty halls, mouldy ceilings, lack of insulation and poor joinery. Ironically, villas were frowned upon by Auckland's early settlers, partly because frowning was more commonplace in Victorian times but also because everyone failed to see that even a modest two-bedroom villa would one day be worth more than the GDP of a small African nation.

THE UNIT

Not a popular choice among aspiring Jafas, probably because the only people who live in units are the elderly, people who need other people to wash them and prostitutes working from home.

THE APARTMENT

Perhaps the biggest problem with buying an Auckland apartment is noise insulation. Many apartments have paper-thin walls meaning you will inevitably gain some appreciation of your neighbours' lovemaking abilities. On the other hand the potential for eavesdropping may be a bonus to some.

THE DREAM HOME

This type of home is often talked about by Jafa homebuyers. Ironically, it does not exist — there are no dream homes in Auckland, only real homes.

LESS COMMON TYPES OF DWELLINGS

THE TINNIE HOUSE

Not made of tin as the name suggests, Tinnie houses are sought after by those with an interest in gardening and recreational drug use. A good Tinnie house can pay for itself through its cash crops.

THE CRIB

Originally an LA phenomenon but increasingly popular in South Auckland, cribs are prized for their **posses** and gaggles of booty-touting **bitches**. Cribs can be rented out as locations to film crews shooting rap and R&B videos, helping pay the mortgage. Drive-by shootings can be a problem.

WHERE TO BUY

A lot of people say the three most important things about buying a home are: location, location, location. In fact, that's only one important thing repeated three times. When buying in Auckland the three most important things to consider are:

1. Where the house is;
2. How close the house is to where you want to be;
3. Where the house is.

FINDING A GOOD NEIGHBOURHOOD

A SIMPLE TEST

It's important to gain a sense of any neighbourhood you hope to move into. Begin by simply walking down the street on which you plan to buy. Once you have made it to the end of the street ask yourself the following questions:

- Has anyone asked me for money?
- Has anyone asked me about Jesus?
- Has anyone offered me oral sex?
- Am I bleeding from anywhere?

If the answer to any of the above questions is 'Yes', the street is probably not in a suitably Jafa neighbourhood.

APPRAISE THE SURROUNDING HOMES

Take a close look at the homes on your prospective street. How have the occupants chosen to expand and enhance their dwellings? Compare the homes in the examples below:

Good Jafa Neighbourhood	Bad Neighbourhood
White picket fence perimeter	White 'Police, Do Not Cross' tape perimeter
Windows bordered with authentic colonial frames	Windows boarded
Three-car garage	Three-car lawn
Large fragrant gardens	Large fragrant 'crops'
When you're away, neighbours happy to feed your cat	When you're away, neighbours happy to feed your cat to their Pitbull

Housing the Jafa

APPRAISE LOCAL BUSINESS ACTIVITY

You want to be sure that the part of Auckland you're considering is on the move. You can gauge this by surveying local business activity. What kinds of businesses are operating in the area? Compare the businesses in the example below:

Good Jafa Neighbourhood

Servilles

Herne Bay Law

ASB Bank

Bad Neighbourhood

Charming Salon 28 Massage

Steve's Used Cars & Anger Management

Sharkey's Insto-Casharama

FIND THE RIGHT-SOUNDING STREET

Don't underestimate the importance of street names to a Jafa. You will need to supply this to many individuals and businesses so naturally you want your address to create the right impression. Compare the street names in the example below:

Good Jafa Street Name

Seafieldview Road

Bad Street Name

Ellerslie/Panmure Highway

Seafieldview Road — The name of this road suggests that either you can see the sea by standing on this field-like road or you can see both the sea and a lovely nearby field from this road. Either way you're winning.

Ellerslie/Panmure Highway — Not only is it a noisy highway coursing with traffic, it doesn't seem to know whether it's in Ellerslie or Panmure. Also, words like 'highway' are associated with words like 'robbery'. So are words like 'Panmure'.

Also bear in mind that the name of your street will determine your child's 'porn name'*.

HOW MUCH SHOULD A HOUSE IN AUCKLAND COST?

Quite often, desirable houses in Auckland do not even come with a price on them. This is because they are priceless. Sometimes houses are so expensive you have to apply just to learn how expensive they really are (this is known as

*You can work out your porn name by taking the name of your first pet and putting it before the name of the first street you lived on. For example, if your first dog was called Boo Boo and the first street you lived on was Strong Street your porn name will be 'Boo Boo Strong'. Note how the name of your street names makes all the difference.

POA — Price On Application). If the application for a POA is accepted, then the buyer is taken into a special room with the seller, the real estate agent and a grief counsellor.

ESTIMATING THE VALUE OF A HOUSE

In order to be able to make a reasonable offer on a property you need to be able to estimate its value. The following is a simple formula that has been known to work.

1. Think of an amount that is at the upper end of what you would reasonably be prepared to pay, if pushed (bearing in mind that prices have risen significantly since you began reading this sentence).
2. Double it.
3. Multiply this by the number of Pajeros or Land Rovers you see parked on the street.
4. Divide this by the number of police cars you see on the street.
5. Double this amount, just to be sure.
6. Add a zero to this amount.

NB: Add 10–12 per cent to this amount for every day that passes from the moment you make your initial estimate.

The above formula will not only give you some idea of a property's value, it will give you some idea of why there is a Third World.

GUIDE TO WHAT YOUR $$$ WILL BUY WHERE IN AUCKLAND		
Amount	Herne Bay	South Auckland
$300,000	a letterbox	a marae
$500,000	a letterbox on a pole	a marae + iwi
$800,000	a house and carport	two houses and an actual port
$900,000	a house and garage	a suburb
$5 million	a house and helicopter pad	Auckland International Airport

A QUICK GUIDE TO SOME POPULAR JAFA NEIGHBOURHOODS ON THE MOVE

CENTRAL CITY

The influx of **Asian immigrants**, mainly students, has turned the centre of Auckland into a booming residential precinct with apartment blocks popping up everywhere like weeds. Indeed, some are about as watertight as weeds. Asian culture has been a colourful addition to the central city with its **restaurants**, **shops** and **massage parlours** offering everything from a traditional Chinese massage to a traditional Chinese blowjob.

GREY LYNN

An area popular with the homosexual community and often referred to as 'Gay Lynn'. Grey Lynn shops and businesses accept **pink dollars** (the gay currency) and enjoy a favourable exchange rate (roughly two to one against the Kiwi). In some parts of the suburb you can still hear **traditional gay code** being spoken. You can also enjoy **gay food and drink**, which is the same as regular food and drink only more expensive and much smaller.

THE VIADUCT

The 'economic hard-on' that followed the America's Cup brought cafés, bars and restaurants to the Viaduct transforming it from a polluted, industrialised and decrepit dockland into a polluted, industrialised and decrepit dockland with bars, cafés and restaurants.

WAIHEKE ISLAND

This gem in the Hauraki Gulf, just 35 minutes from downtown Auckland by ferry (three hours by dredge), used to be a community of **hippies** and feral cats. Nowadays the cats are mostly domesticated and the hippies are feral but the island is no longer the exclusive haven of alternative lifestylers. Rich Jafas from the mainland discovered the island in the 1970s as a perfect getaway, attracted by its vineyards, **secluded beaches** and relaxed attitude to wife swapping.

JAFA HOME FENG SHUI

Good home feng shui

Bad home feng shui

SOME IMPORTANT FEATURES YOU MAY WANT IN YOUR JAFA HOME

Roof — An often overlooked feature. Is it the right colour? Is it in the right place? Does it have a helicopter pad?

Garage — An essential feature of any Jafa home. Is it large enough to adequately house one or more Land Rovers? You can test this by driving a large 4X4 into the garage. If the vehicle smashes into the siding, the garage may be too small.

Bathroom — Is it big enough to support any future renovations such as the installation of a flotation tank and a bidet, or in the case of West Aucklanders, a beer fridge?

Backyard — This can be an advantage if you decide to subdivide or need to bury bodies at short notice.

North facing — This refers to the positioning of the property. The obsession with facing north is because Auckland's poorer suburbs are to the south and Jafas prefer to be facing in the opposite direction to their poorer cousins. Muslim Jafas may be more concerned as to whether the property is Mecca facing. With increasing numbers of Muslim immigrants arriving in Auckland, a **Halal house** may be a wise investment.

Sea views — Jafa homebuyers seem to be obsessed with sea views, as if the sea is going to evaporate some time soon and they want to make the most of it. In cities like Tokyo smart people just buy a big painting of the ocean and save millions.

ONCE YOU OWN A HOUSE IN AUCKLAND

Not long after you have purchased your home you should have it revalued. Make a note of the capital gains you have made on the property and then make sure you point this out to as many people as possible, at every single opportunity that arises. Stating and restating the amount you have theoretically made on your property is a form of positive reinforcement that helps psychologically ease the burden of the crippling debt that is your mortgage.

RENOVATING

Renovating in Auckland used to be carried out by homeowners themselves in what has always been a great Kiwi tradition. Nowadays few Jafas renovate themselves, choosing instead to have the work carried out by a **home make-over reality TV show** such as *DIY Rescue* or *Mitre 10 Changing Rooms*. This is made easier by the fact that all Jafas are either freelance TV producers or know someone who is. Advantages of having your home redecorated by a television show include:

- You get to meet Petra Bagust;
- TV tradesmen arrive up to 30 times faster than regular tradesmen;
- All heavy moving is sped up and set to a jaunty theme tune;
- The whole thing takes just one commercial half-hour.

For those who decide to do their own renovations, here are some pointers.

QUICK TIPS FOR JAFA DIY RENOVATING

SAFETY FIRST

The best safety tip we can give you is to consult your partner before beginning renovations. Some of the worst Jafa DIY injuries actually result from a lack of communication between spouses. This, and the presence of sharp-edged power tools.

DEMOLITION

The act of demolishing a house, or parts thereof, provides you with the rare opportunity to legally enjoy vandalism. But professional help may be required and this can be costly. A cheap demolition option is to host a Westie stag party and then make sure that the stripper never turns up.

FENCING

Choose a fence that compliments you, your family and the threat level of your neighbourhood. Before taking down an existing fence ask yourself: 'Why am I unhappy with this fence?', 'How long will it take to install the new one?' and 'What breed of dog am I now exposing my family to?'

SOUNDPROOFING

A cheap and popular way for Jafas to soundproof their homes is by having good neighbours. **Pensioners** are the most effective form of soundproofing because they don't make any noise and they can't hear any noise generated by you. They are also clean, low maintenance and easy to install. A good lining of pensioners should be at least two houses deep in order to provide you with a 'people and noise buffer'. You may need to re-soundproof your home every five to 10 years due to strokes.

7 EMPLOYING THE JAFA
FINDING A JOB IN AUCKLAND

GETTING BY IN AUCKLAND

It's a sad fact but one needs money to survive in Auckland. In New Zealand we at least enjoy the benefit of a social welfare system, which is more than can be said of other Third World nations. In some parts of the country entire families can survive on the **dole**, or 'unemployment benefit' as bureaucrats colourfully call it. The unemployment benefit is designed to highlight the benefits of unemployment. This is something entire generations of Kiwis have grown to appreciate. But if you're serious about making it in Auckland, the dole will not be enough. It will not even be close to enough. Trying to survive on the dole in Auckland is like trying to walk on the moon wearing nothing but a nice pair of slacks and a polo shirt. You're going to have to learn how to stand on your own two feet — possibly for hours on end if you decide to work in retail.

HOW TO MAKE FAST MONEY IN AUCKLAND

There are many ways to make a quick buck in the city. Some require you to have skills and qualifications. Some require you to possess talent. Some require you to let strange people do things to you. Let's begin by considering some of the immediate options for the new arrival to Auckland.

BECOME A HUMAN STATUE

Becoming a human statue is a great way to get paid for literally standing around and doing nothing. Human statues remind us why we invented statues in the first place. The ancient Greeks understood that statues, like today's robots, could literally stand in for humans — liberating us from the toil of having to stand around indefinitely. But for some strange reason, certain people will still pay money to watch someone do nothing for hours on end. Even if they are fully clothed. Becoming a human statue may seem easy, but the industry has been plagued by trouble. In 1994 city-wide strikes brought human statues to a standstill. Nobody noticed. It's still unclear whether the strike has finished or not — as human statues are unable to comment.

Human statue pros	Human statue cons
Work your own hours	Being covered in paint can cause a rash
Get paid for doing nothing	You cannot move to scratch yourself without losing artistic credibility

BECOME A BUSKER

Busking is something the new arrival can do almost as soon as he or she gets off the plane, bus or train. It is a good way to showcase your talents to a wide range of people, including potential employers. Even if you have no demonstrable talents you can still make it as a busker because if you are that bad, people will pay you to shut up.

Busking pros	Busking cons
Work your own hours	Only one step up from begging
Work close to public transport	
Complete lack of talent no barrier to success	

BECOME A BEGGAR

Many beggars are former buskers who had their instruments stolen or realised their playing was inhibiting their ability to attract an audience. Begging is not as simple as it looks. It requires both confidence and a total lack of pride.

Begging pros	Begging cons
Work your own hours	Choices severely limited because beggars can't be choosers
Get paid for doing nothing	Relies on the kindness of others, which doesn't count for much in Auckland
Get to sleep on the job	

BECOME A PROSTITUTE

For many years prostitution or 'whoring' was frowned upon but in 2003 legalised prostitution came to Auckland. Many opposed legalisation, fearing that professionalism might erode the spirit and pride synonymous with the amateur era. However, since turning professional the world's oldest profession has become a viable career option for young people. 'Prostitution' now sits between 'prosthetic limb designer' and 'pro-wrestler' on the list of jobs shown to Jafa school-leavers. Auckland's polytechnics now offer training in everything from the basic pleasuring of another person to large-scale commercial brothel keeping or **pimping**. In Auckland, there's never been a better time to get on the game.

Prostitution pros	Prostitution cons
Work your own hours	Having to commit unspeakable acts sometimes a problem
You get to make up your own professional name, like 'Candy'	
Spend a lot of time in BMWs	
Get to meet the Auckland Blues	

GETTING A REAL JOB

If you've read this far, you're obviously serious about making it in Auckland and actually becoming a Jafa. It should be obvious by now that making it in the big city requires a serious commitment to work. If you got caught on 'Become a Human Statue' or the bit on prostitution, then frankly you're not what we're looking for in a reader. The preceding text was just a test to sort the contenders from the pretenders. If you've got this far you're obviously a contender. Or you jumped a section. Perhaps you were interrupted by someone wanting you to do the dishes or just focus on your lovemaking. If so, go back to the front of the chapter and begin again.

WHERE TO LOOK FOR A REAL JOB

If you want to look for a job in Auckland, buy a newspaper. Take the unemployment section and roll it into a sturdy rod. Now beat yourself with it. Beat some sense into yourself because you are never going to find a job through the newspaper, unless you are prepared to answer ads beginning: 'Escorts, no experience required.' The only way to get a halfway decent job in Auckland is through word of mouth.

WHAT IS WORD OF MOUTH?

Word of mouth is finding out about a job through word of mouth; that's why it's called 'word of mouth'. This should not be confused with 'use of mouth', which is a way of securing a job favoured by some Jafas.

APPLYING FOR A JOB

Once you have found a job you are interested in you must start to piece together a job application. This will typically include your CV, some references and a covering letter.

COVERING LETTERS

A covering letter is essential to any job application in Auckland. It's called a covering letter because it should 'cover' all the inadequacies you have that make you unsuitable for the job. It should also cover your true intentions with a series of generic platitudes that make you sound like a highly motivated and yet harmless individual who is unlikely to cause any trouble. You should not be too frank. The following is an example of how NOT to write a covering letter.

Employing the Jafa

THE TRUTHFUL COVERING LETTER (NOT USUALLY EFFECTIVE)

June 4 2004

Dear Sir/Madam,

I would relish the opportunity to join your dynamic team and believe I could blend in as just another faceless employee, contribute little and ultimately leave when it suits me to pursue more lucrative opportunities overseas.

I see your company as an ideal stepping stone to a career in a much more glamorous industry. I am therefore highly motivated to work in your office just long enough to amass a small cache of stolen office stationery, earn a reference and save enough money to fuel my drug habit. My proactive, can-do approach would enable me to take advantage of all non-toll-barred phones to call friends overseas. I would utilise my extensive computer skills to download objectionable material via your company's broadband connection and I would look forward to applying my passion for human resources by sleeping with as many impressionable young office juniors as possible.

Furthermore, my well-honed acting skills would allow me to maintain the pretence that I actually give a shit about the X industry whilst all the time secretly resenting my superiors and back-stabbing them at the office Christmas function before getting very drunk, questioning your sexual orientation to your face and then assertively downsizing my personal dignity by getting caught having sex with the temp on the boardroom table.

I look forward to meeting you in person so I can lie about my background and experience to your face at a mutually convenient time.

Yours truly,

J. Jafa

THE UNTRUTHFUL COVERING LETTER (USUALLY VERY EFFECTIVE)

June 4 2004

Dear Sir/Madam,

I look forward to joining your team, especially as I have photographs of you being intimate with someone who did not appear to be your marital partner.

Yours truly,

J. Jafa

YOUR CV AND HOW TO ENHANCE IT

If your covering letter doesn't do the trick then you will need to have a good CV. The best way to enhance your CV is by what's called 'embellishment'. Another word for this is 'lying'. This is a process whereby Jafas simply create an employment history to suit the job for which they are applying. Consider the example below.

WHAT YOU SAY YOU DID	WHAT YOU DID
Oversaw traffic flows on one of Auckland's busiest thoroughfares	Worked at McDonald's drive-thru
Worked in advertising	Delivered circulars for *The Warehouse*
Worked extensively in the community	Did 300 hours community service for shoplifting
Single-handedly disarmed a terrorist cell, defused a bomb planted in a crowded shopping mall and freed 15 hostages — on more than one occasion.	Spent six months on the dole playing PlayStation Counterstrike
Was a key figure in Auckland's professional rugby scene	Streaked at the Blues versus Hurricanes Super 12 semi-final

Using the same principle, your personal qualities and characteristics can be used to make you sound very employable. Consider the table below.

PERSONAL QUALITIES CITED	ACTUAL PERSONAL QUALITIES
Forward and assertive	Have anger-management issues
Can multitask	Have Multiple Personality Disorder
Not afraid to say what I think	Suffer Tourette's syndrome
My presence in the workplace is always felt	Have weight problem
Creative with language	Compulsive liar
Happy to work through lunch breaks	Anorexic
I believe that what you get out is what you put in	Bulimic
Committed, motivated and driven	Addicted to P

HOW TO IMPRESS A JAFA EMPLOYER AT A JOB INTERVIEW

THE BASICS

CREATING THE RIGHT IMPRESSION

How you dress, groom and handle yourself at a job interview is part of your 'packaging'. This should not be confused with your 'packed lunch', which is different (and relates to men only, hopefully). Dress in a manner that befits the company and the nature of the position for which you are applying. As a rough guide you should dress like you are going to a funeral and yet still hoping to pick someone up. If you elect to wear a 'power suit' endeavour to make sure it is not more powerful than the one worn by your interviewer (this may be construed as cocky).

Appropriate interview attire.   Inappropriate interview attire.

OVERCOMING NERVES AT THE INTERVIEW

If you become nervous during the job interview, a good technique to calm yourself is to imagine your interviewer naked. This often helps you relax provided you DO NOT BECOME DISTRACTED BY THIS TRAIN OF THOUGHT. In the rare event that your interviewer is actually naked, imagine them clothed. If these techniques fail, imagine yourself naked. If all this nakedness is causing unwelcome physiological reactions, imagine Helen Clark naked.

USING THE INTERVIEWER'S NAME A LOT

In the course of your conversation with the Jafa interviewer it is important to make frequent use of the interviewer's first name. This personalises the interaction and creates a relaxed and friendly air that could not otherwise be created without the use of powerful stimulants such as Ecstasy. Go one better by undertaking some research before the interview to find out any nicknames the interviewer might go by. This extra touch can really add sparkle to an otherwise routine exchange, as in the example below.

INTERVIEWER: So, where do you plan to be in five years?

YOU: Well, Bruce, I plan to have made middle management within five years so that I can order around people who are up to three times more intelligent than me. Know what I'm getting at, Mr Floppy?

The interviewer will probably be amazed that you called him 'Mr Floppy', given that this is a name used only by his wife. However, this can only encourage positive feelings and could be the difference between you and the next applicant.

ADVANCED TECHNIQUES FOR IMPRESSING AT A JOB INTERVIEW

GENTLY PROBE FOR ANY NEPOTISM YOU CAN EXPLOIT

When it comes to finding a job people often say: 'It's not what you know, it's who you know.' This is certainly true of Auckland. New York may have six degrees of separation but in Auckland it's 0.6 degrees of separation. Statistically, it's possible, if not likely, that you share a colleague, friend or even wife with your interviewer. A lot of people would view this as potentially embarrassing but a previously unknown connection is a good opportunity to establish a rapport. For example: 'Yes, Janet and I were lovers for several months. She spoke very highly of you,' or 'Hey, wasn't your daughter porking my brother?' With a few well-chosen words an instant connection is forged.

MAKE YOURSELF APPEAR SOUGHT AFTER

Have a friend call the interviewer on his direct line during the interview and ask for you. This will make you seem in demand.

ADD A LITTLE MAGIC

When your interviewer asks: 'Can I see a more detailed CV?', it's always nice to be able to say: 'Look in your top pocket.' A simple magic trick like this can help make a tense interview more relaxed and enjoyable.

TAKE NOTES DURING THE INTERVIEW

Jotting things down as the Jafa interviewer drones on suggests you value thoroughness, have application and are professional. At the end of the interview surprise your interviewer by handing him a piece of paper headed 'Ten Things I Like About You.'

JAFA JOB INTERVIEW WORST-CASE SCENARIO TEST

This short test may help you prepare for any unforeseen challenges that may arise during the job interview.

1. You notice your interviewer has his fly down. Do you:
   a. Ignore it
   b. Ask if this is company policy
   c. Politely and discreetly point it out, then ease the tension by recalling an amusing anecdote about a time when you were flying low
   d. Using deft sleight of hand, attempt to zip him up without him noticing
2. Your interviewer asks you a question you have absolutely no idea how to answer. Do you:
   a. As a diversion, point out that he is flying low
   b. Say, 'I'd like to answer that question with a question,' then ask what the hell he's talking about
   c. Admit you don't know the answer but make up for this by demonstrating your general knowledge of miscellaneous facts such as: 'Did you know that the dolphin is the only other animal that has sex for pleasure?'
   d. Clutch a hand to your chest and feign a massive heart attack
3. You arrive for an interview only to find that you recognise your interviewer from a one-night stand you once had. Do you:
   a. Act like you don't recognise them
   b. Immediately acknowledge the incident and make out you had not previously and have not since known such pleasure
   c. Suggest the interview be relocated to a room at the Metropolis Hotel
   d. Ease the tension with a line like: 'Well, I guess I've already passed my physical'
4. You arrive for an interview and to your embarrassment find that you are wearing the exact same outfit as your interviewer. Do you:
   a. Tell them it looks much better on them
   b. Start mimicking their actions perfectly so that they believe they are looking into a mirror, then, when they finally fall asleep, sneak away and get changed
   c. Excuse yourself to the toilet, then quickly dye all your clothes another colour in the sink
5. You've lied in your CV about attending Harvard University. It turns out the interviewer attended Harvard and starts asking you questions you should know the answer to. Do you:
   a. Tell them it was actually Härvärd University in Sweden
   b. Tell them you attended Harvard in the late 1920s and you just look really good for your age
   c. Explain that by 'attended Harvard University' you mean you attended an anger management seminar in one of the lecture halls

6. The interview starts and because you are so nervous, you vomit on the table, then seconds later you involuntarily defecate in your pants. Do you:
    a. Put a gun in your mouth and pull the trigger
    b. Immediately stand up and proclaim, 'And that's exactly what I think of this company's competition!'
    c. Take out your portable time machine and rewind time to five minutes ago
    d. Start urinating on your interviewer — what the hell? You've already vomited and shat your pants
7. Your 65-year-old interviewer starts unbuttoning their clothing and tells you, 'There is *one* way you can be sure you get this job'. Do you:
    a. Walk out. The job isn't worth it
    b. Go for it. If they're 65, they've probably got a few tricks up their sleeve
    c. Start scratching your groin and say, 'Sure, you give me the job, I'll give you pubic lice... sounds like a fair trade to me'
    d. Tell them you'd be happy to but you just had 'the op' and the stitches haven't quite healed yet and by the way, they would not *believe* what they made your new genitals out of.
8. The interviewer has unsightly burn scars on their face, which you can't stop looking at. Do you:
    a. Say, 'Jesus mate, that's hideous. Accident at the company barbecue?'
    b. Quickly take out a lighter and burn your own face so you can proceed with the interview on an equal footing
    c. Make light of their disfigurement by saying, 'Hey, you know they can cover that with skin grafts from your arse cheeks, eh?'
    d. Distract yourself by staring fixedly at their breasts/crotch instead
9. The interviewer starts choking. Do you:
    a. Perform the Heimlich manoeuvre
    b. Perform the '1812 Overture'
    c. Go right up to their face and tell them you won't help them unless they give you this goddamn job!
10. The interviewer is just in the process of offering you the job when he/she spontaneously combusts. Do you:
    a. Throw them to the ground and smother the flames with your own body
    b. Throw them to the ground and smother the flames with someone else's body
    c. Walk them, flaming, into the main office and make them repeat the bit about you getting the job before they perish
    d. Film them burning and sell the footage to as many overseas home video shows as you can. You may never have to work again

ANSWERS 1) D 2) C 3) D 4) B 5) A 6) B 7) B 8) D 9) C 10) C or D is acceptable

IMPORTANT 'DO NOTS' AT THE JOB INTERVIEW STAGE

If asked to explain why you left your previous job, avoid using lines like, 'God told me to do it'. In fact, DO NOT use the word 'God' at all unless you are pointing out that God spelt backwards is 'dog' — as this is mildly interesting.

Employing the Jafa

DO NOT comment on the spouse and/or children pictured in your prospective employer's family photos. If the interview has gone well, you may become overconfident. It's easy to unwittingly drop your guard. Next thing you know you're looking at a photo on your interviewer's desk saying, 'Is that your wife in the bikini? Man, she looks like one sweet lay; no wonder you've got so many kids.' You may mean well but inevitably something is lost in the translation.

DO NOT wink at your potential employer and say, 'You *won't* be sorry if you take me on... I think you know what I mean.'

DO NOT get overfriendly and start telling your potential new boss the joke about the guy with the robot hand that finishes with the punchline 'Fuck me!' and you slapping your arse with your hand.

ONCE YOU'VE GOT THE JOB

Having been offered the job you probably think you're home and hosed but if you are going to be working for a big Auckland company, there is likely to be some mandatory testing before you are signed on. The **psychometric test** is the most common form of employee testing in Auckland. It takes its name from the original corporatese word 'psycho-metric' (literally, to 'measure a psycho') and is designed to ascertain whether or not you are a psycho. If the results show that you are a psycho you may be culled from the pool of applicants or, if you are applying for the position of bouncer, you may go straight onto the shortlist.

These days psychometric testing is used as a standard recruitment tool by every major organisation from Microsoft to Al Qaeda. For example, here is an example of a psychometric test from the Al Qaeda human resources department.

23. If 3000 infidels enter a building at 9 a.m. but 500 take their hour-long lunch break at 12.30 p.m., how many are blown up if a large bomb goes off at 12.52 p.m.?
   a.   About 2500, God willing
   b.   Not enough
   c.   God is great!

Believe it or not the correct answer is C, which illustrates the point that different employers look for different things in their employees.

WAY OF THE JAFA

GAINING PROMOTION

Once you've got a job in Auckland the first thing you will want to do is think about how you can get a better one. The best way to do this is through promotion. No self-respecting Jafa expects to gain promotion simply by working hard in the same job for years. This would take so long that the eventual benefits of promotion would mean nothing by the time they reached a position to enjoy them. For instance, many young men fantasise about having sex with their own gorgeous young secretary. However, by the time they have been promoted to a position where they can hire a 19-year-old secretary they are so old they can no longer achieve or maintain an erection except in the presence of a qualified medical specialist. Clearly, climbing the Jafa corporate ladder is all about skipping a few rungs.

SLEEPING YOUR WAY TO THE TOP OF THE CORPORATE LADDER

Jen the Jafa says:
'Why do all that work when you can just do the boss?'

Of all the routes to the top, the *Way of the Jafa* recommends the root to the top. Sleeping your way to the top of the corporate ladder is the best way to fast-track your career as well as being a great way to get to know people. The Jafa school of thought on this matter is increasingly realistic about the need to 'screw the crew' or 'dip one's pen in the company ink' in order to climb the corporate ladder. An aspiring Jafa's likely success in this area depends on both the 'crew' and the length of the corporate ladder they are climbing. With increasing numbers of women now in the workforce, the prospects for workplace romance are better than ever and must be exploited. Such an approach may seem cynical and inconsistent with the core values of hard work and honesty upon which this country was built. That's because this is Auckland we're talking about, not New Zealand.

PROCEDURE FOR SLEEPING YOUR WAY TO THE TOP OF THE CORPORATE LADDER

1. Identify person in a position of power and influence.
2. Seduce person in position of power and influence.
3. Ask for a raise or promotion.
4. Demand a raise or promotion.
5. Threaten to tell all if you do not receive a raise or promotion.
6. Repeat.

SLEEPING YOUR WAY TO THE TOP — STEPH'S STORY: A NEW ZEALAND TOWEL SERVICE ODYSSEY

Ever since I was a little girl I've always wanted to work for the New Zealand Towel Service (NZTS). It was the motto that got me: 'The New Zealand Towel Service — There's So Much More to Us Than Towels'. I devoted every spare minute I had to towels and towelling-related activities. All my hard work was rewarded when I gained a lowly position in the 'inwards goods' department of the NZTS. My career trajectory seemed assured. But it wasn't easy at NZTS. The cauldron of corporate towelling was more intense than I had anticipated. After a year languishing in 'inwards goods' I began to notice other people being promoted ahead of me. There seemed to be no justice. Then one day, when I felt at my absolute lowest, I accidentally walked in on Mr Wyatt, our general manager, having sex with Julie from accounts. I was so shocked by what I saw, I ran to the bathroom and cried into the two-ply standard (our most popular towel, 100 per cent double-woven cotton for superior strength and durability). I later asked Julie what she had been up to. 'To get to the top you sometimes have to get on top,' she told me. It was then that I decided I was prepared to do what it takes to get to the top. Suffice to say I am now the West Auckland district manager for the New Zealand Towel Service. I oversee the distribution of over 3000 metres of towelling in more than 200 cafés, restaurants, bars and businesses every week. It would have taken me years to get here if I had simply waited my turn. Sleeping my way to the top has not been easy; it has cost me two relationships and one unwanted pregnancy but I don't have any regrets. When I watch the NZTS vans rolling out of the supplies bay I know that my vision and drive, as well as all those afternoons with Mr Wyatt, has got me to where I am today.

Jeff the Jafa says:
'I'm all for women being on top in the workplace, in fact, it's my favourite position.'

SLEEPING YOUR WAY TO THE TOP: ONE MAN'S STORY

Dear Forum,

It was the Friday before Christmas and I was working late photocopying the monthly accounts at the office. I was just about to finish up when my boss Jenny surprised me. She was standing in the doorway, one hand twirling her long chestnut hair, the other resting on her shapely hip. Jenny was our regional manager, a fit 39-year-old divorcee with a real zest for life. She was wearing her usual superbly fitted power suit and absurdly high heels. She asked if I would mind helping her with some 'personal' photocopying. I said sure but was flabbergasted when, without warning, she slipped out of her skirt revealing her perfectly ██████ ████████. She jumped onto the photocopier and ████ her gorgeously sculptured legs across the still warm glass. I tried to concentrate on the monthly accounts still to do but my ████ had already become as ███ as algebra. Jenny told me to push the 'copy' button so I extended my hand only to have her stop me. 'With your ███,' she demanded. As she was my boss, I had no choice but to obey her. I slipped off my Hugo Boss executive slacks, revealing my by now ███ █████████ ███. Jenny had already shed her jacket and bra revealing full and firm ██████ and ████ ██████. As I pressed the 'copy' button the flash of the photocopier's bulb momentarily blinded me. When I regained my sight I saw that Jenny was on her knees. She took my ██████ and rubbed it against her ███ ██████ before taking it in ██ ████ little ███. I was in heaven as she adroitly ██████ my love ███████. She held my ███ in her left hand and stroked the base of ██ ████ with her right, all the while slathering the ██ with the moistness of her ██ eager ████. Like the professional she was, Jenny brought me close to ████████ several times and then, with a gentle squeeze, she tipped me over the edge into an oblivion of ecstasy. Watching her flowing chestnut locks cascading over her petite feminine shoulders as she bobbed up and down, her beautiful █████ █████ ██ swaying alluringly, was just too much. I finally ███████ ████ her velvety ████████ of pleasure. Jenny thanked me for helping her with the photocopying and speedily dressed. 'Good to see you putting in the overtime,' she said with a wry smile as she sashayed out the door. Even though I was soon promoted to senior sales manager with my own PA, I always insisted on doing my own photocopying and Jenny was always willing to help.

Name and address withheld

WORK AND STRESS

Some people think it's important to 'work from a place of rest' rather than 'rest from a place of work' but there's no reason why your workplace can't be a place of rest. Managing work stress is critical to your survival in Auckland and the best way to do this is to remove the 'work' from the equation. Studies show that when you reduce the amount of work you do, the 'work stress' just falls away. According to the *Way of the Jafa* the best way to approach work is to avoid it. This is called getting your 'work to work for you', rather than you working for it, or 'killing time on the job'.

HOW TO KILL TIME AT WORK

All Jafa employees need to learn how to kill time in the corporate world. This is entirely different to 'time-wasting', which is something done by the unemployed and students. Killing time is about the effective, preconceived use of paid time to avoid doing real work, allowing you to while away the empty hours in between the times when, through no fault of your own (e.g. deadline pressure), you actually have to do some work.

NEVER START WORK IMMEDIATELY

Although you should always arrive for work on time it is important that you DO NOT START WORK IMMEDIATELY. Statistics show that while Jafas who start work as soon as they arrive at the office get more done, they suffer more stress and injuries than Jafas who spend the first three hours of the day downloading and forwarding amusing animated emails. Work is the same as any other activity; it requires you to warm up properly first. To gently ease into your work you should have a time-consuming ritual and observe this every working day. Consider the example below.

THE JAFA 22-STEP WORK WARM-UP

1. Arrive at work.
2. Walk to your desk, being careful to take the longest route possible.
3. Turn on your computer.
4. Sit down.
5. Adjust your seat to make sure it is supporting your back.
6. Perform a few work injury prevention exercises.
7. Go to the coffee room to make your first cup of coffee for the day. While there, have a 20-minute conversation with a workmate about some TV programme that was on the night before.
8. Return to your desk. Search for your favourite pen.
9. Ask if anyone has seen your favourite pen.

10. Search the office high and low for your favourite pen; this may take some time. If anyone asks, point out that it has sentimental value and you can't focus on work until you know where it is.

11. Attempt to send a group email around the office about the missing pen and spend the next half-hour working out how to actually send a group email.

12. Call the IT department and talk at length about how to send a group email.

13. Follow up call with a visit to the IT department.

14. Once back at your desk, adjust the position of the family photos on your desk so that they catch the light as it is at that exact moment. If anyone asks, explain that this is important for 'motivation'.

15. Go to the toilet.

16. Read the paper. Begin with the business section (it is important to know what is going on in the industry). Then read every other section followed by any graffiti on the inside of the toilet door. Using a vivid marker, respond to any graffiti as you see fit.

17. Return to your desk, being careful to take the longest route possible.

18. Reboot your computer.

19. Tidy your desk. It should now be time for lunch.

20. Go to lunch.

21. After lunch be careful not to start work immediately.

22. Go back to step 2 and repeat as necessary.

GENERAL TIME-KILLING THROUGHOUT THE WORKING DAY

CHECK YOUR EMAILS/USE THE INTERNET

Check your emails every hour and be sure to reply to every message, even ones slugged: 'Get enlarged and give her the pleasure she deserves' or 'Do you want pictures of big hard black men sent to your in-box *every day*?' You can also surf the Internet under the guise of research. If surfing for porn make sure the content is in some way work-related, e.g. www.officesluts.com.

CHECK YOUR PHONE MESSAGES

This can take up entire hours, especially if you are expecting an important call. If you leave your desk, even for a minute, you may have missed the call. For this reason you must check your messages. You do this by dialling into your phone. Often you may discover there are no new messages of any importance. You hang up thinking you have checked your messages. However, that all-important call could easily have come through while you were checking your messages, thus necessitating you check your messages again. And so it goes on. This also creates the impression that you are continuously engaged in business over the phone, one of the most corporate poses any Jafa can assume.

MAKE COFFEE

Coffee is the all-important prop that keeps people going in the corporate world of Jafas. The *Way of the Jafa* teaches that you should consume at least six cups of coffee every day. Making coffee is a great time-killer because every time you make a cup, office etiquette dictates you must offer to make one for each of your fellow employees in the immediate vicinity. Be sure to make a list of each person's preferences when you are taking orders but DO NOT KEEP THIS LIST. Make a new list each time you offer to make coffee. This eats up more time.

ON-THE-JOB JAFA SKILLS THEY WON'T TEACH YOU AT UNIVERSITY OR POLYTECH

Many tertiary institutes train their students in the work skills required for specific jobs in the corporate world. Few, however, actually teach their charges those essential skills that will be required of any Jafa working in any Auckland office regardless of their job. What follows is a brief guide to often overlooked job skills that all corporate Jafas should master.

PHOTOCOPYING YOUR GENITALS

Like any sane person, the first thing that goes through the corporate Jafa's mind when they see a photocopier is that they should immediately photocopy their genitals. In some offices people photocopy their faces believing this to be amusing enough, but it's only a matter of time before one of your fundamental apertures is rendered to white A4 in powdered ink. When photocopying your genitals take extra care so as not to break the photocopier's glass. This can be both an expensive and physically dangerous mistake to make. Be sure to get your genitals as close to the glass as possible in order to ensure the most detailed rendering but at the same time do not rest your full weight on the photocopier. You can achieve the right balance by sitting on your hands and using the strength of your wrists to take some of your body weight (Fig. 1). Do a test copy first. Adjust contrast levels as necessary. Once you have safely photocopied your genitals you can have great fun with your workmates trying to guess which photocopy belongs to whose genitals and indeed what kind of genitals they depict.

Fig. 1: Photocopying your genitals. Men may wish to make use of the 'enlarge' button, while many Jafa women prefer to 'reduce'.

TRANSFERRING A CALL

Highly expensive research undertaken for this book has shown that no matter how much training someone receives or how much practice they get, they will never be able to transfer a call from one phone to another without cutting off the caller at least 86 per cent of the time. For Jafas, the figure is closer to 98 per cent. For this reason you should NEVER TRY TO TRANSFER A CALL. To be safe you should probably NEVER ANSWER A PHONE.

SIGNING A WORKMATE'S GOING-AWAY CARD

The novelty-sized going-away card is a long-standing tradition of the Jafa office. Many workplaces observe this tradition every Friday because there is always someone leaving their dead-end job in Auckland for a dead-end job in Sydney or London. All Jafas need to know how to contribute to a going-away card. Signing someone's going-away card is not an easy thing to do. You may be called on to do this at short notice, giving you little time to come up with something pithy. Or you may hate the person who is leaving for always taking your stapler. Nonetheless, it's important that you be able to think fast and still come up with a comment that is warm, supportive and complimentary. Whatever you say, it should be appropriate to the occasion. Consider the examples below.

INAPPROPRIATE GOING-AWAY CARD COMMENT

Dear Jacinda,

I really enjoyed working alongside you. You have the best arse on the third floor.

Love Jake

APPROPRIATE GOING-AWAY CARD COMMENT

Dear Jacinda,

You've helped make a sometimes dull job all the more bearable. I'm sure your new company will benefit tremendously from your superb arse.

Regards Jake

HOW TO CONDUCT YOURSELF AT A JAFA BUSINESS LUNCH

In most parts of New Zealand the average lunch break runs to about one hour but in Auckland there is such a thing as the Jafa Business Lunch (JBL), sometimes referred to as a 'liquid lunch'. Adding the word 'business' to 'lunch' usually adds hours to the length of the luncheon engagement. It soon becomes a business lunch, afternoon tea, drunch, dinner and nightclub or strip joint. The JBL is one way corporate Jafas use their work as a cover for their alcoholism. Booze is the lubricant for most, if not all, business done at JBLs, therefore Jafas need a good working knowledge of wine so they can order by **alcohol content**.

DRINKING: Your drunkenness needs to be carefully moderated so that your level of intoxication builds gradually. If you peak too early, you may be too drunk to enjoy the rest of the meal or you may regurgitate it prematurely. If you are not drunk enough, you may not react naturally when your boss comes on to you.

CONVERSATION: The main point of a JBL is to **avoid talking about business at all costs**. Actually discussing business can get in the way of enjoying the meal and negates the need for further business lunches. Immediately stymie any attempt to discuss business by starting your own casual conversation. Begin with broad, uncontroversial subjects everyone can relate to, e.g. 'How 'bout those bloody immigrants?' Avoid controversial or contentious subjects that may cause tension, e.g. who should be All Blacks coach or captain. Later, move on to more pertinent subjects such as which people in your office you would like to sleep with. Take care not to mention anyone from the office that is actually at the lunch. From this point on it should be easy to avoid the danger of doing any work at all and the lunch is free to drag on for hours.

JAFA BUSINESS LUNCH TIMELINE GUIDE

If the general protocol of a Jafa business lunch is properly observed, it should resemble the following series of events:

2 p.m. — Arrive at restaurant for your 1.30 p.m. booking. Order drinks.

2.20 p.m. — When approached by waitress, ask for more time to consider the menu. Order drinks instead.

2.55 p.m. — Begin discussing important issues concerning you at work, such as, is it just you or does Simon from marketing smell really bad?

2.56 p.m. — Apologise to Simon from marketing, whom you didn't realise was at the table. Order more drinks as a diversion.

3.30 p.m. — Discuss which of the waiting staff you would like to sleep with.

4.20 p.m. — Commence flirting with Matt/Julie (or similar) from accounts. Order Matt/Julie (or similar) a cocktail.

5.10 p.m. — Insult boss. Instantly regret gaffe. Order drinks as a distraction.

5.15 p.m. — Reapply for your job.

6.20 p.m. — Drunkenly confess to Matt/Julie (or similar) from accounts what you would like to do to them.

7.30 p.m. — Graphically illustrate to Matt/Julie (or similar) from accounts what you would like to do to them by using a bread stick and some dip.

4 a.m. — Actually do to Matt/Julie (or similar) what you'd like to do to them, back at Matt's/Julie's/your flat. Realise you do not want to do it after all.

4.05 a.m. — Vomit.

4.10 a.m. — Lose consciousness.

6.00 a.m. — Get up for work. Apologise to Matt/Julie (or similar) from accounts.

10.00 a.m. — Arrive at work.

10.02 a.m. — Hide in toilet.

12.00 p.m. — Repeat.

Even if you manage to sleep with important people, balance your time-wasting with your work and participate fully in the rituals of the Jafa office, there is still no guarantee of your survival. For this reason you need to be prepared for unexpected challenges.

BEING ASKED TO GET DOWN FROM THE CORPORATE LADDER — DEALING WITH REDUNDANCY

Because the corporate world of Auckland is what Jafas call 'cut-throat' or 'dog eat dog', it is quite possible you may at some point face **redundancy**. Being made redundant is a fearful prospect for most Jafas climbing the corporate ladder, but, like anything, it's how you deal with it that counts. There are three main approaches to dealing with redundancy in the Jafa workplace.

1. The American Approach
2. The Kiwi Approach
3. The Jafa Approach.

THE AMERICAN APPROACH

Also known as 'going postal', the American approach involves obtaining a firearm (preferably semi-automatic) and mowing down several of your fellow employees, including the person who fired you. You then remain holed up in your former workplace until police arrive.

Pros	Cons
Sends an extremely clear and unambiguous message to your employer that you are not happy about being made redundant	Your next job will likely be the position of 'Bitch' working under someone called 'Snake'

THE KIWI APPROACH

The Kiwi approach is what most people do when made redundant. You simply accept your fate and ask for a reference. A going-away gathering takes place in the boardroom on your last Friday and you are presented with a novelty-sized going-away card containing wholly inappropriate humorous comments from your workmates and the odd smiley face. You may receive a gift, such as a cup in the shape of a bosom. The following Monday you get on the dole after telling everyone you left your job to 'pursue other challenges' (such as working out how to get the dole under more than one name).

Pros	Cons
You retain your reputation as a sane person	Get paid 1952 wages on the dole

THE JAFA APPROACH

If you have been adhering to the *Way of the Jafa* you will have done what it takes to get ahead without actually doing any work. You may have slept with several important people or made an effort to find out which important people have slept with which employees. Now is your opportunity to make good on your inside knowledge by bribing your boss for a generous redundancy package.

Pros	Cons
Golden handshake allows you to support yourself while you take a six-month holiday in Ibiza	You will never work in this industry again (this can easily be a pro too, depending on the job)

8 EXERCISING THE JAFA
HEALTH AND FITNESS

Health, beauty and vitality are the three pillars of the Jafa holy trinity of physical well-being. That said, beauty is by far the most important of the three because beauty can create the *appearance* of health and vitality. This is why the *Way of the Jafa* teaches us that the way to health and vitality is through starving oneself in the pursuit of beauty.

DIETING — HOW TO STARVE YOURSELF TO GOOD HEALTH

The average Jafa female now rates 'dieting' above 'eating' on her list of things she could never give up. At any given time up to 80 per cent of Auckland women are on a diet. Experts believe up to 90 per cent of the remaining 20 per cent may be bingeing, having failed as part of the other 80 per cent. Of the 300-plus published diets currently available, 78 per cent of Jafa women have tried more than 50 per cent and as many as 42 per cent have tried all 300. Only 2 per cent actually lose weight.

SUCCESSFUL DIETING

The success of a diet depends almost entirely on how many people the Jafa female tells that she's on a diet. The more people she tells, the more this reinforces the reality of the diet, even if she hasn't altered her eating habits at all. And if she simply tells people she's on a diet, regardless of whether its true, they will be forced to compliment her on how slim she's looking, which is all the Jafa female wanted out of the diet in the first place. This applies equally to Jafa men.

CHOOSING A DIET

When considering embarking on a trendy Jafa diet, always **consult your doctor** first. To do this you should make a doctor's appointment, turn up and then read all about the latest diets in the women's magazines available in the waiting room. Bear in mind that some of these magazines may be up to 20 years out of date so it's important to sort the old-school diets from the more up-to-date ones. 'Dr Atkin's Revolutionary All-Lard Diet' was considered cutting edge in the late 1970s but times have changed.

ACHIEVING BALANCE

The success of a Jafa diet should not be measured by weight loss alone but by 'before' and 'after' photos, too. Successful diets depend on a proper balance of diet, exercise and **trick photography**. To make the results of the diet more impressive a 'before' photo should be taken in an outfit that resembles, as closely as possible, a tent. Posture is also critical. A PRONOUNCED SLOUCH must be maintained for the photo along with an UGLY SCOWL. When the diet has either run its course or been abandoned, an 'after' photo should be taken. The subject should always WEAR BLACK, stand side on and use make-up that emphasises the cheekbones. When the photos are shown to other Jafas, they will be forced to remark on the difference. If the above technique fails, then just Photoshop your head onto Nicole Kidman's body.

BUT WHY DO I NEED TO LOOK BEAUTIFUL?

Why is it that Jafas spend so much time trying to lose weight in an effort to achieve some impossible physical ideal? This is a question many novice Jafas ask of the *Way of the Jafa*.

Many social commentators also question Jafa society's obsession with beauty. While it is important that these issues are raised, it is more important to remember that without beauty Jafas would have no gauge of a person's worth. Auckland's entire value system would collapse, causing anarchy and chaos. Without standards of beauty Jafas would have no way of differentiating newsreaders from transvestite prostitutes, for instance. This fact is often overlooked in debates about society's beauty obsession.

Some people suggest that beauty is only 'skin deep' and that what really matters is 'inner beauty'. In fact, inner beauty is mostly irrelevant because it cannot be seen with the naked eye.

A BRIEF GUIDE TO POPULAR JAFA DIETS

As a general guide any diet that has the word 'low' in its name, such as the Low Carbohydrate Diet, is considered the way to go. Here are some popular Jafa diets.

THE LOW SELF-ESTEEM DIET

For years Jafas have understood the appetite-suppressing benefits of maintaining a low self-esteem. Feelings of failure, worthlessness and general emotional fragility (such as those that may arise after a break-up) are embraced by users of this diet. Depression encourages loss of appetite which reduces food intake resulting in massive weight loss depending on how much they liked the person who dumped them.

THE LOW DIET DIET

Particularly popular with young Jafa women, the Low Diet Diet consists of many different diets and works best when the user gives up on one diet and then starts a new one at least twice a week. Changing diets like this to keep up with Jafa dieting trends leaves virtually no time to settle down and actually eat anything, thus encouraging weight loss, and if you are single, date loss.

THE P-DIET

Increasingly in vogue, the P-Diet is based on a controlled daily intake of pure methamphetamine. Pure meth is one of nature's most effective appetite suppressants. If properly abused it can dramatically aid weight loss, although it has been linked with unfortunate side effects such as a pronounced desire to chop your neighbours' arms off or murderously rob old people.

THE ETHIOPIAN DIET

Although generally acknowledged as being devastatingly effective, the Ethiopian Diet is not a popular choice among Jafas. It calls on the user to move to sub-Saharan Africa, immerse themselves in a bloody ethnic conflict raging across drought-stricken plains and eat nothing but Red Cross-supplied rice gruel until Bob Geldof holds an internationally broadcast rock concert in their honour.

THE LIVER-CLEANSING DIET

The liver is carefully removed and polished with a special cloth. Many experts debate the health benefits of this diet.

OBESITY

Despite obsessive dieting among many Jafas, obesity is a growing epidemic in Auckland. Statistics show that up to 35 per cent of Jafas are 'clinically obese', more than 50 per cent are 'overweight' and at least 67 per cent have 'let themselves go'. Jafa health experts warn of the 'on-flow' effects of obesity on Jafa society — the presence of just one fat person in an Auckland street can lower the rate that house prices increase in that street by up to 1 per cent. Obesity results in the death of 360 Jafas each year: most die of embarrassment at the gym or at the beach.

EXERCISE

Exercise is an essential accompaniment to any diet because when properly overdone it can cause vomiting, thus aiding further weight loss. Before embarking on any exercise programme you should consult your doctor by a leaving a note under the windscreen wiper of his Mercedes. Jafas should also consult their partner, their personal stylist, their life coach, and if they are joining a Jafa gym, their bank manager.

Exercising the Jafa

GYMS

Gyms outnumber churches in Auckland by three to one, which gives us some indication of how important exercise is to the Jafa — or possibly what godless, image-obsessed heathens they are. Indeed, the standard of physical fitness and attractiveness required just to enter a Jafa gym is so high that prospective gym-goers must first pass a rigorous training programme devised by former Olympic athletes and modelling agents.

JOINING A JAFA GYM

Before you can join a Jafa gym you will be expected to undergo a fitness test. This will assess whether or not you are fit to be part of the Jafa gym culture. The Jafa Gym Fitness Test will assess your:

Involuntary Muscular Reflex — Your ability to repel unsolicited come-ons in the gym changing rooms;

Aerobic Capacity — Your capacity to withstand repeated doses of ultra-fast kiddie-pop aerobics music;

'Self-Reflexability' — Your ability to maintain eye contact with yourself in the mirror while lifting heavy weights;

'Cardio-fiscular Fitness' — The rate at which you burn money; this can affect your ability to afford the monthly gym subscription;

'Lycratic Tolerance Index' — Your tolerance for Lycra (both wearing and observing).

WHAT TO WEAR TO THE GYM AND HOW TO WEAR IT

It is very important to avoid wearing restrictive clothing when attending a Jafa gym. Gym-going Jafas, both male and female, avoid this problem by wearing clothing so small it can only be detected with an electron microscope. To ensure this clothing does not in any way restrict their movement or the view of their twitching buttocks, female Jafa gym bunnies do their utmost to actually physically absorb their clothing. This rules out any kind of restriction when they are performing elaborate aerobics manoeuvres such as bouncing and smiling. When the correct bodily absorption of microscopic clothing such as leotards is successful, the Jafa woman achieves a state known as **anal floss**.

SHOULD I WEAR MAKE-UP AT THE GYM?

No self-respecting Jafa woman would be seen dead without make-up (in Auckland, even corpses are impeccably made up). Just because you will be exercising does not mean you should risk someone actually catching a glimpse of you as God intended. However, because you may be exercising, the amount of make-up you wear to the gym should be limited. Foundation should be no more than 3 centimetres thick and eyeliner should be kept to a minimum (just one eye). Some Jafa women choose to apply extra mascara, however, as the added weight can help work out the crucial eyelid muscles.

The right clothing is essential at a Jafa gym.
Wear a leotard, a unitard or like this woman, a retard.

A QUICK GUIDE TO EXERCISE AT THE JAFA GYM

CARDIO

Cardio is short for 'cardiovascular', which is the medical term for trying to improve your fitness by deliberately having a heart attack. Cardio machines in a Jafa gym are usually coupled with television sets suspended from the ceiling. These play music videos featuring people the cardio machine users are trying to look like. One drawback of cardio machines is that users have little to show for their efforts. No matter how hard they go, no matter for how long and no matter how many miles they clock up, they will still only ever be in the gym.

Jen the Jafa says:
'Attending a gym is the best way to lose weight. My gym subscription cost me so much I could no longer afford food. I lost 16 kg in three weeks.'

WEIGHT MACHINES

There is a reason time spent at the gym is called 'working out', this is because much of it will be spent working out how to use the weight machines. It's easy to spend half an hour on a machine only to discover it's actually a photocopier.

FREE WEIGHTS

These weights are not free. Not even the small ones that look like something that just fell off your car. What 'free weights' actually means is 'without assistance'. And in a Jafa gym that's exactly how it happens. No matter how awkward and dangerous your lifting technique, you will not receive assistance from anyone.

SAFETY FIRST: HAVE SOMEONE SPOT YOU

When using weights at the gym the Jafa will sometimes have another gym user 'spot' them. By lifting very heavy weights and making a lot of clipped, guttural noises the Jafa attempts to attract the attention of other gym users who will 'spot' them and hopefully be impressed by what they see. It is also considered polite to show your appreciation for the facilities by grunting and moaning. As a general rule, men grunt and women moan.

SWIMMING

Swimming and its sister activity drowning are very popular at Auckland's beaches, especially those on the West Coast. Jafa gym-goers use training pools to train for beach swimming. It should be noted that swimming in a pool is completely different to swimming in the ocean. The flutter board will not help you prepare for the swells of Piha, unless while swimming you have someone beat you with it.

SWISS BALL

The Swiss ball is often held up as an example of what a neutral country can achieve when not focusing on arms production. There are various ways to use a Swiss ball. People are made to balance it, balance on it, bounce it, bowl it, sit on it, lay under it, stand next to it, jump off it or stroke it gently like an embalmed pet. They are now available in almost every size and colour and have provoked spin-offs such as the Swiss Army ball, the Swiss Egg, the Austrian Sphere and the less successful Mexican Cube.

PERSONAL TRAINERS

The Jafa personal trainer's job is highly technical — it involves pointing you in the direction of a gym machine and then counting the number of repetitions you do on it. Some personal trainers can't actually count but provide expert motivation by saying things like: 'Come on, that's it... yeah. Awesome!' If you're really serious about personal training you can now hire personal trainers who have their own personal trainers to personally train them while they personally train you. This is why Jafa gyms are so crowded. It is not uncommon for Jafas to use these professionals outside the gym for personal training in shopping, dieting and self-pleasuring.

A BRIEF HISTORY OF JAFA FITNESS FADS

JAZZERCISE

By the early 1980s scientists had established the potential benefits of combining the word 'exercise' with other words that carry a positive connotation. Dr Johan Gorman, an Auckland University biolinguist, first combined the words 'exercise' with 'jazz' accidentally whilst trying to invent a new word to describe the blue lint that forms balls in a man's belly button. 'Jazzercise' was born. The benefits of the new 'Jazzercize' were immediately obvious when tested on humans, chief amongst them being that you could make videos of it using washed-up former TV presenters and sell them in their truckloads.

PILATES

Pilates was invented by the German fishmonger Joseph Pilates. Whilst engaged in sexual intercourse with his wife, Pilates devised a way to be able to view his wife's buttocks without leaving the missionary position. It was the first time anyone had achieved this without the use of mirrors. The flexibility developed by these German lovers resulted in the birth of a whole new discipline of exercise and launched a thousand infomercials (and some astonishingly athletic babies).

POWER WALKING

Power walking was invented by extremely indecisive Jafas — unable to decide whether they wanted to run or walk. In the course of their dilly-dallying a new form of public humiliation was inadvertently created. The main benefit of power walking is that it is so humiliating its exponents can lose weight through sheer embarrassment alone.

TAI CHI

An age-old Chinese discipline derived from the playing of martial arts movies in slow motion, Tai Chi manipulates 'energy centres' to promote health and vitality. Unfortunately, it only works on Chinese people.

YOGA

Yoga is an elaborate Indian discipline for stretching the liver and breaking wind. It was originally devised by Indian teenagers as a means of swapping ideas about sexual positions without their parents knowing. Today there are different schools of yoga but all are taught by 'gurus' — elderly Indian men whose main job is putting pressure on young women's 'chakras'.

Jeff the Jafa says:
'Yoga changed my life. Before I couldn't even touch my toes. Now I can not only touch my toes, I can scratch my back with them.'

WAY OF THE JAFA

Yoga has been so popular among Jafas that it has achieved 'cross-over' appeal. Several of the discipline's most famous poses, such as the 'wet dog' and the 'prancing lizard', went on to become popular dance moves in the nightclubs of the 1980s and 1990s. As a form of exercise, the chief benefit of yoga is that women can learn to cup their breasts using the soles of their feet (Fig. 2), while men may develop the ability to fellate themselves (Fig. 3). This may explain yoga's increasing popularity among Jafa men.

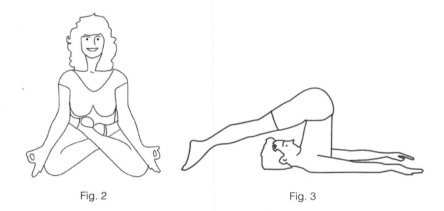

Fig. 2   Fig. 3

9 ENTERTAINING THE JAFA
RECREATION IN AUCKLAND

'Recreation' was once a byword for 'procreation' in Auckland. Less than a generation ago Jafas had few options in the way of entertainment aside from recreational sex. Today, thanks to legalised prostitution, recreation is still closely linked to procreation (see 'Sex' later in this chapter) but thankfully there are literally tens of other things to keep Jafas occupied as well.

THINGS TO DO IN AUCKLAND

THE SKY TOWER AND SKY CITY CASINO

At 328 metres high Auckland's Sky Tower is not the world's tallest structure but as there are no other very tall buildings in Auckland it is widely acknowledged as being the **world's most incongruous landmark**. The original brief given the Sky Tower's designers was to build something 'demonstrative, distinctive and ideally very similar to a part of the male anatomy'. Despite not being more specific the results were magnificent. When the tower was finally finished Jafas everywhere knew that Auckland had acquired one of the world's most well-endowed landmarks.

The Sky Tower collected a string of international design awards including the Frank Lloyd Wright Award for Outstanding Industrial Design and the Sigmund Freud Memorial Award for Cock-shaped Buildings.

The Sky Tower's flagship restaurant is the **Southern Hemisphere's only five-speed revolving restaurant**. The complex has four forward gears and one reverse gear allowing diners the chance to see five times more of Auckland whist enjoying a three-course meal, if they can hold down that much food.

Each year in June the Sky Tower sees a mad dash from its base to its observation deck. The city's fittest athletes race up the 1276 steps to the top of the tower as part of the ever-popular **Skyrun Dash for Cash Challenge**. A big prize goes to the casino-goer who can lose the most money in the space of time it takes the first runner to sprint from the bottom to the top of the tower. The record stands at $24,580 in just 12.4 minutes (set in 2002 by an unemployed solo mother). For a more adrenaline-pumping option why not consider actually jumping off the Sky Tower? **Skyjumper** is a professional service run by the casino that offers an alternative to the Auckland Harbour Bridge for those who lose everything in the casino and decide to end it all.

AUCKLAND FILM FESTIVAL

Auckland's annual film festival starts in July and presents a smorgasbord of award-winning films from all over the world. It's also a great opportunity to see top-quality **pornography masquerading as art**. Each year the organisers are sure to include a scintillating selection of poorly made but arty flesh-flicks that specialise in using 'thematically challenging' material as an excuse for showcasing often beautifully rendered depravity. Films that are banned everywhere else have been known to turn up at the festival and despite annual protests from the **Society for the Promotion of Outright Fear and Ignorance Through Outdated Values** (SPOOFITOV), these always screen to full houses.

IMAX

Originally hailed as the 'number one' Auckland movie experience **Imax** lived up to its billing by attracting crowds numbering one for any given screening (including the projectionist). Imax offered a new format to directors and Hollywood quickly embraced the medium, taking complete crap to new heights. When Imax opened one reviewer commented, 'It was amazing. At one point I actually felt like I could reach out and punch the actors.'

Shut down for some time, Imax has enjoyed a small revival through screening adult foreign movies. *Das shagniem von Brunhilde (The Deflowering of Brunhilde)* proved particularly popular with its target demographic of white single males over the age of 35 and still living at home, and now screens nightly.

The **Rugby World Cup** provided another opportunity for Imax to shine but when the All Blacks lost it proved devastating in more ways than one. Losing to Australia was hard enough but to watch it on a screen seven storeys high was, for many Jafas, just too much.

AUCKLAND ZOO

Auckland Zoo is one of the city's finest attractions. It houses perhaps the best collection of **animals that have gone insane due to captivity** in the Southern Hemisphere.

Feeding time at Auckland Zoo; a hippo enjoys an extra-strength latte made from its mother's milk.

AMERICA'S CUP BOAT CRUISE

The NZL82 boat cruise prides itself on giving punters a taste of the **real life experience** of Team New Zealand's 2003 America's Cup Defence. As well as enjoying sailing on the harbour, participants get to bail water out of the aft deck just like they did on NZL82 in the America's Cup Final. For an extra $120 you can even experience the sensation of being showered in carbon-fibre filings when the mast snaps.

Jen the Jafa says:
'Sure, Wellington had Lord of the Rings but we had the America's Cup and that is so much more impressive than a plain old ring. I mean it doesn't even have a diamond in it.'

CONSEQUENCES OF AUCKLAND LOSING THE AMERICA'S CUP

- Property prices drop (for about 15 minutes)
- Dramatic reduction in the incidence of Jafa women saying: 'Hello, sailor'
- Hauraki Gulf dolphins finally able to enjoy quiet time
- Pete Montgomery forced to yell at wife, kids, instead of TV viewers
- Auckland's nickname officially changed to 'City of Not Quite So Many Sails'.

THE AMERICA'S CUP IS NO LONGER AUCKLAND'S CUP

The loss of the America's Cup was a huge blow for the Auckland region. Not only did the syndicates and tourists leave town in droves, but an order for 200,000 America's Cup-shaped novelty kettles had to be cancelled at the last minute. Many blamed a lack of organisation, a lack of funding and a lack of Russell Coutts. However, now that the smoke has cleared it's obvious the real reason Team New Zealand failed was because its boat barely floated and eventually snapped like a toothpick in one of yachting's most spectacular own goals. It quickly became evident that Team New Zealand had not only 'pushed the design envelope' but had burned down the factory that made the envelope (the 'design envelope' metaphor has since been phased out of Kiwi yacht-racing parlance). Many non-Jafas criticised the America's Cup for being the sole preserve of rich business tycoons but that may now be changing; an Auckland-based challenge has been announced by WINZ as part of its 'sail-for-the-dole' scheme. Long-term unemployed will be flown to Europe for the 2006/7 regatta, where they will receive an accommodation allowance and on-board training as part of a campaign based around a revolutionary boat made entirely of plastic recycled from old Community Services cards.

Fotopress

NZL82's mast snaps mid race. It turned out to be a double blow, not only did it knock Team New Zealand out of the race but the mast was just out of warranty.

WAY OF THE JAFA

Roller-spading is a popular Jafa pastime that combines
skating and posing to create a new way of picking up strangers.

THEATRE

Auckland does not have a thriving theatre scene when compared to that of
Wellington but live theatre nonetheless attracts a loyal following at a handful
of venues including **Showgirls** and **The Las Vegas Strip** (Show and Tell
Night, Mondays).

RAINBOW'S BEND

Auckland's only true theme park, Rainbow's Bend houses the **Southern
Hemisphere's most extensive collection of antique amusement park
rides**. Test your courage on ageing roller coasters and other thrilling rides,
which, due to tighter safety regulations overseas, are no longer in service
anywhere else. The 1960s vintage **180-degree cinema** specialises in 'surround
film' classics — including the Zapruder film — see the assassination of John F
Kennedy on a three-storey 180-degree screen — said to be an experience just
like being there (parental guidance advised).

THE WAITAKERE RANGES

The number of criminals that have confessed to dumping bodies in the
Waitakere Ranges tells you something about the splendid isolation of

this pristine bushland near Auckland's West Coast. The remoteness of the 'Waitaks', as they are affectionately known, also makes them a popular choice among naturists but this should not deter birdwatchers or trampers. Unfortunately, many of the area's native bird populations have been decimated by possums but a variety are still routinely sighted including the **Sparrow**, the Grey Sparrow, the Brown Sparrow, the Grey/Brown Sparrow, the Spotted Sparrow and the rare Sparrow-shaped Sparrow.

THE BEACH

Auckland's beaches are among the most beautiful in the world and are held close to the heart of most Jafas. Not only are they calm, sheltered and ideal for swimming but they also act as a natural detoxification plant for the city's **raw sewage**. There are many different types of beaches in Auckland: surf beaches on the West Coast; swimming beaches on the East Coast and a number of **specialist beaches** including nudist beaches and gay beaches. Gay beaches are the same as other beaches except body hair is strictly forbidden (except on women where it is compulsory).

The Auckland City Council places very strict controls on the use of recreational marine vehicles. By law, jet skis must be the latest model and must be highly visible at all times to meet strict posing standards.

WAY OF THE JAFA

THE ROYAL EASTER SHOW

Each year Auckland plays host to The Royal Easter Show, an exhibition and carnival that boasts the Southern Hemisphere's best collection of **former state-sponsored instruments of torture that have been converted into amusement park rides**. A perennial favourite is the *Hurricaner*, which exposes thrill-seekers to 8 Gs of centrifugal force as it spins at up to 120 km per hour — a unique experience in the physics of motion and occasionally a unique experience in semi-digested hot dogs.

OTARA MARKET

South Auckland's largest and most bustling market is a favourite with locals and outsiders alike, especially anyone who has just been burgled and would like to buy their home-theatre system back.

AK03 AND AK05

In 2003 Auckland finally got its own Arts festival. The festival proved once and for all that while Auckland had absolutely no arts scene, this could be fixed by importing artists from overseas at great expense. Unfortunately very few people attended the festival despite heavy promotion. Research later showed that while everyone knew about AK03, most people thought it was a semi-automatic machine gun.

SEX

The legalisation of prostitution has seen Auckland embrace the sex industry. Whoring is now a legitimate Jafa profession and pastime. Once ladies of the night, Jafa prostitutes are now also ladies of the morning, lunchtime and mid-afternoon. They often work from home or from one of the increasingly popular mobile brothels now operating, such as *Door to Door Whore*.

Although criticised by the moral minority, legalisation has seen standards improve. Today's professional sex workers are more competent with intelligent, informed conversation. Topics depend on the university degree the sex worker is paying off. Being legal, Auckland prostitutes now add GST to their charges but also offer a discount for students, pensioners and Community Services cardholders as well as a two-for-one deal on Tuesdays.

Entertaining the Jafa

Since the legalisation of prostitution in 2003, these streetwalkers
no longer have to disguise the fact that they're actually men.

The legalisation of the sex trade has been a boon for the unemployed.
Work and Income New Zealand plans to move up to 10 per cent of Auckland's
unemployed into the sex industry in a new scheme entitled 'Root for the Dole'.

SKIING

Skiing is a sport that is of very special significance to the *Way of the Jafa* — it provides the only known reason for Jafas to venture south of the Bombay Hills.

A BRIEF GUIDE TO JAFA SKIING

USE THE RIGHT GEAR

The first rule of Jafa skiing is to make sure you have the appropriate equipment and clothing. It is essential that your gear be no more than one season old. Any older and you run the risk of **gear failure** (when your gear fails to be fashionable, putting you and Jafas around you in danger of embarrassment). **Visibility** is essential on the slopes. All labels (Burton, Salomon, Helly-Hansen) should be clearly visible to others at all times.

A typical mountain Jafa. This woman's gear cost a total of $6000, board and boots excluded.

NEVER SKI ALONE

No Jafa skier should ever ski alone. If you ski alone you run the risk of having no one around when you pull off your best moves on the slopes. With no one there to witness your efforts you gain no credit for your ability. Skiing is expensive, so every expedition must in some way enhance a Jafa's reputation. Always ski with others.

ALWAYS TAKE YOUR CELLPHONE

Jafas always have cellphones handy when skiing. A cellphone means someone will always know where you are, especially when you ring them at the office to report on how much you are enjoying yourself.

KNOW HOW TO STOP

Effective stopping is perhaps the first skill all Jafa skiers must master. The key to effectively bringing yourself to a stop is to leave it until the absolute last possible moment so as to maximise your speed, then turn very sharply on your skis or board in order to create the largest possible **snow-spray**. This is the best way to effectively announce your arrival and skill level.

A GUIDE TO AUCKLAND NIGHTLIFE

BARS AND CLUBS

Auckland Central RSA is a great place to go if you enjoy hearing war stories told by octogenarian alcoholics (which is why locals refer to it as the 'Returned Stereotypes Association'). One of the few Auckland establishments still serving beer by the gallon, the in-house **TAB** allows punters to bet on sports, racing and who will be the next regular to fall off his stool.

Firerisque, an all-night cave club, was allowed special dispensation from the city's fire regulations because of its location right next door to the Auckland Central Fire Station. However, this counted for little during the last fire in 1997, as most of the firefighters were in the club and heavily intoxicated at the time. The sounds on offer here include Big Beats, Techno, House, Hard House, Deep House and occasionally music, too. The action usually continues right up to sunrise or until the DJ collapses, whichever comes first.

Auckland's premier rock venue, **The Crypt,** is ground zero for Heavy Metal, Thrash Metal, Death Metal and on Thursday nights, Norwegian folk music. Visiting big name overseas rock stars have been known to show up at The Crypt — Pearl Jam's Eddie Vedder vomited on the upstairs bar and **Kurt Cobain** is said to have considered killing himself here.

Cuju's is popular with tourists and expatriates, and is perhaps best known for its ethnic theme nights. Every Wednesday is **Brazilian night**, featuring Brazilian music, dancing and pubic hair grooming.

The Palladium is Auckland's only **eight-level club**. The fact that seven of the levels are car parks does not seem to deter a loyal clientele.

The Loaded Pogue is frequented by a more youthful crowd, it proudly boasts a clientele of the city's **youngest drinking-age girls**. Unfortunately this means the clientele also includes the city's oldest single or recently separated men. The happy hour (5 p.m.–2 a.m.) is unique in that it is followed by an 'unhappy hour' when drinks are normal price but the chance of them being spiked is greatly enhanced.

My-Thai Karaoke Bar specialises in Thai-style karaoke and music. Enjoy traditional northern-style Thai cuisine while taking in authentic **Thai-style karaoke**. The music here is so authentic it was recently described as 'the most unholy racket ever unleashed on human ears'.

Karaoke-Doki is Auckland's premier karaoke bar and seats up to 300 with more than 200 singers presented on any given night. A number of **major Kiwi stars** were 'discovered' here, including Hayley Westenra, K'Lee and the woman from the Briscoes ads.

The Wang family is proud to be running East Auckland's biggest traditional Irish pub — **O'Wangahans.** This historic but contemporary venue is famous for its food, especially the popular #68 Beef and Blackbean Irish Stew. The facility boasts Auckland's only Zen garden bar and hosts the city's only bilingual pub quiz (English/Mandarin). It is also believed to have the best feng shui of all Auckland's Irish pubs.

GAY BARS AND CLUBS

Gaybo's is a massive three-level complex and claims to be the '**gayest club in the Southern Hemisphere**'. Officially, heterosexuals are not allowed unless they are certifiably 'bi-curious'.

The **Island of Lesbos** is one of the city's few outdoor gay venues, it consists of a tent erected on the traffic island at the Royal Oak roundabout on the third Friday of each month. A popular hangout with Auckland's **Clitterati** and motorists.

JAFA BOUNCERS

At some time during your night out in Auckland you are going to come into contact with a Jafa bouncer and it's important to know how to approach one. Bear in mind that the job of bouncer is the only occupation where Cromagnon man can still find regular employment. The Jafa bouncer's job is, at least 90 per cent of the time, the same as the job of a retaining wall (indeed most Jafa bouncers resemble these). There is no point in trying to talk your way past a bouncer, as the following table clearly illustrates.

What You Say	What the Bouncer Hears
I just want to see if my friends are in there.	Blah blah blah
I was just in there, remember?	Blah blah blah
I'm with the group you just let in.	Blah blah blah
Don't you normally do the gay clubs?	Let's fight now.

A typical Jafa bouncer. The earpiece connects the wearer to an on-call anger management counsellor.

A BRIEF NOTE ON HOLIDAYING

New Zealand's only Jafa-friendly places (where it is considered safe for Jafas to holiday) are the **Coromandel** and parts of **Queenstown** (as these are considered unofficial suburbs of Auckland). The rest of New Zealand is considered 'Jafa hostile' and should not be visited without first notifying the New Zealand Embassy in Canberra or your mum.

10 RAISING THE JAFA
NURTURING THE JAFA YOUTH

There is no doubt that the need for better parenting in Auckland is more acute than ever. Every day we read reports of violence, drug abuse, unwanted pregnancies, even suicide. And that's just the parents. In the highly competitive Auckland of today, good parenting can be the difference between raising a captain of industry and raising a captain of the Paremoremo Prison Touch Rugby Team.

BRINGING A JAFLING INTO AUCKLAND — CHILDBIRTH THEN AND NOW

In 19th-century Auckland Jafa women had many more babies, mainly because pioneer women were trying to raise an entire country from scratch. In colonial times an Auckland woman would have a baby about as often as she had sex (this was how physicians first discerned a correlation between the two events). Men were more fertile in those days and birth control was primitive (the chief form of contraception was the girdle).

Statistics show that today's Aucklanders are having fewer babies than ever. Jafa women are choosing a career over a baby because careers are easier to dress for and generally involve fewer stretch marks. Because Jafa women have so few babies, a great deal of fuss must be made about each birth and each baby. Having a baby is, for a Jafa woman, right up there with being the first in the country to take delivery of the latest 3 Series BMW or having a *Shortland Street* star turn up to their dinner party.

JAFA CONTRACEPTION

The Pill is easily the most popular form of contraception among Jafas. The Pill, or Ecstasy as it is sometimes known, is used daily by many Jafa women. Also known as E, the Pill is the perfect contraceptive because when the Jafa female takes it she is gripped by an overwhelming desire to dance to horrible music played by young men being paid more than a brain surgeon to play their record collections, whilst surrounded by masses of sweaty strangers who she may eventually give neck rubs to. All of this constitutes an overwhelming distraction from actual sexual intercourse with her partner.

HOW MANY CHILDREN SHOULD WE HAVE?

This is an age-old question that all Jafa couples must consider when starting a family. Traditionally, the number of children a couple had depended on religion. Protestants tended towards restraint (two or three children) whereas Catholics had as many children as they could think up biblical names for off the top of their heads (usually between 30 and 40).

Today, Jafa family planning is much simpler. Jafas determine the ideal size of their family by the size of their car. They do this using a theorem known as the **Jafa Theory of Relatives**, which states that the natural size of a family decreases in relation to the size of that family's car. For example, if the family car is something like a 5.0-litre 2004 model Land Rover, the natural size of the family will be around 1.5–2.0 children. On the other hand, if the family car is a small or medium-sized vehicle, such as a 1974 Toyota Cressida, the family will naturally comprise between 12 and 18 children. The Jafa Theory of Relatives is demonstrated by the illustration below.

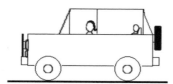

The Jafa Theory of Relatives states that the size of a family
is directly disproportionate to the size of that family's car.

WHAT KIND OF CARE?

For the term of the Jafa pregnancy and ultimately for the birth itself, the Jafa couple must decide what kind of care they will have. In most cases they decide to hire every possible kind of healthcare professional money can buy. These can include:

THE GP

Your family doctor is very important. They initiate a key process that begins with them charging you $50 to refer you to others who will charge you a great deal more. Try to enjoy visiting your GP; it's the cheapest part of the process.

THE MIDWIFE

The Jafa midwife visits once a week to assess the position of the baby and the ongoing financial position of the mother. The Jafa midwife will also constantly measure the tummy of the Jafa mother and recommend ways she can reduce her unsightly bulge through diet, exercise or massively baggy clothing.

THE MIDHUSBAND

A recent addition to birth care in Auckland, the midhusband visits the couple once a week to see how the impending Jafa father is coping with his impending lack of freedom. The midhusband will drink beer and watch sport with the father and occasionally measure the size of his penis, which commonly shrinks through lack of use during pregnancy.

THE SPECIALIST

The Jafa specialist specialises in all aspects of birth care. A good specialist has specialised to such a point that he is able to charge thousands of dollars for simply inserting his finger in the Jafa mother's vagina and saying: 'Hmmmm, that all looks fine.'

THE PERSONAL TRAINER

The personal trainer gives the expectant Jafa mother a fitness regime that will keep her looking taut and terrific before, during and after the birth. The personal trainer may also give the unborn child exercises to do as well.

THE PLASTIC SURGEON

Plastic surgeons are consulted as soon as the mother learns she is pregnant. The surgeon will get to work on 'de-emphasising' the bump and pre-emptively removing the stretch marks before they occur.

THE INTERIOR DESIGNER

Not a healthcare professional, but essential for planning the very latest décor for the 'baby's room'.

THE EVENT MANAGER

Event managers are vital to the planning of both the birth itself and the stressful arrangement of appointments to see the above professionals.

THE PR CONSULTANT

It is vital for Jafas that everyone knows about the impending arrival, so the PR consultant can help with arranging baby showers, dinner parties, notifying the media and arranging exclusive deals with women's magazines.

WHAT KIND OF BIRTH?

These days a Jafa woman has a range of choices to consider when giving birth. In Auckland just having the baby is seen as inadequate if not lazy. The *Way of the Jafa* decrees that the method of birth reflect a given philosophy on child rearing. The three most popular methods of birthing Jaflings are:

- The Water Birth
- The Home Birth
- The Birth Birth.

THE BIRTH BIRTH

The 'birth birth' is the first choice of expecting mothers in South, West and East Auckland. It is a process in which the mother simply gives birth with the minimum of fuss and gets on with life, often within a couple of hours.

THE WATER BIRTH

Adherents of the water birth philosophy believe it fosters more athletic, co-ordinated and balanced children. However, it has also been linked with fostering children who resent their mother for apparently trying to drown them at birth. The water birth has different meanings to different types of Jafas. In Central Auckland it is a very expensive procedure carried out in a controlled environment. In West Auckland the most common form of water birth occurs when a woman goes into labour at the Henderson Public Pools.

THE JAFA HOME BIRTH

Home birthing is a very popular trend among central city-dwelling Jafas. Having a baby at home is regarded as the most natural and organic way to have a child (second only to dropping it in a rice paddy — known as a 'peasant birth'). A home birth gives the mother what is known as the **home advantage**. This is the benefit, often talked about in professional sport, of having your own supporters in attendance on your own turf. The home advantage provides the extra edge that motivates the mother to dig deep and produce her best possible performance. This can really make a difference when you're trying to push something the size of a watermelon through something the width of a cocktail straw.

HOW TO HAVE A HOME BIRTH

A home birth is all about creating the ideal environment through which to bring your Jafling into Auckland. Everything that the child will experience in those crucial first few moments may affect its ability to grow into a healthy Jafa. Nothing can be left to chance. Here are some basic guidelines.

1. Buy a home in which to have the child (ideally, a converted villa or bungalow).

2. Get pregnant. The child must be conceived through an act of love or, if that fails, through sex. Both parents should have eaten nothing but organic food for the last two years or they risk conceiving a normal child.

TURNING YOUR HOME BIRTH INTO A FUN SOCIAL OCCASION

There's no reason why the birth of your child should be an overly sombre and clinical occasion. Many Jafa mothers elect to have home births partly so they can maintain their reputation for entertaining even as they are giving issue to human life. Friends and family gather and may even take part in the procedure.

CHOOSING THE RIGHT PERSONNEL FOR A SAFE AND FUN HOME BIRTH

A doctor or specialist should always be present at the home birth, not just for supervision but for the benefit of the mother's single female friends. The doctor should be both a paediatrician and available. The seating arrangement should allow for him to be seated next to any of the Jafa mother's eligible female friends. Likewise, a wet nurse should be seated next to any single male Jafa friends to complete the ideal boy/girl arrangement.

When it comes to the traditional midwife or matron Jafas prefer what's known as a **matron'de**. A matron'de is a fully trained matron and qualified midwife who can also prepare and serve organic hors d'oeuvre to your guests during the birth. With everyone seated and being served snacks and drinks it's a good opportunity for the mother to regale her guests with amusing anecdotes about her pregnancy while everyone waits for the baby. A brief Powerpoint presentation may help pass the time until the first contraction. **Music** should be used to set the right tone. This should be bright and social enough for entertaining and yet calming and welcoming for the baby. Recordings from the natural world are favoured, especially aquatic ones, such as the sound of waves lapping, whales singing or endangered seals pleasuring themselves.

Jen the Jafa's handy tip:
'Baby products that aren't organic can be made organic simply by putting the word "natural" or "organic" in front of them.'

LABOUR AND BIRTH

Once labour has commenced the mother is lowered into a pool of lemon-scented Evian water which should be about the same temperature as the mother (i.e. no warmer than Judy Bailey's earlobes). Whilst in the pool the mother indulges in some light aqua-yoga, which releases tension on her three main 'chakras' or pressure points (her hair, her mother and her husband or boyfriend). When the mother begins dilating she is removed from the water. Fresh organic **basil** is applied as a natural antiseptic and to give proceedings a fashionable Italian flavour. At this point the Jafa mother may receive a full facial and preliminary make-over to reduce the effect of any unsightly puffiness. A beautician may perform a **Brazilian section** as an aesthetic preparation for further dilation.

When the baby finally arrives it is not slapped by the doctor as this is seen as unduly violent and out of step with current Jafa thinking. Instead the infant receives intensive psychological **counselling** to help it get in touch with its inner child and any issues arising from a bad foetushood. This continues until the child begins to cry. The infant is then swathed in organic hand-picked cotton wool and smeared with organic avocado oil before being presented to the mother on an organic woven-flax bowl (this should have been made by a woman no less than two-thirds Maori).

DEALING WITH PND

Many Jafa mothers will inevitably suffer from PND (Pre-Natal Depression). Pre-Natal Depression results from the dawning realisation, late in a woman's first pregnancy, that she will never be as slim, petite or delicate as she was before her pregnancy. While the Jafa mother welcomes the temporary increase in breast size, PND reinforces the sobering thought that her breasts will soon turn into pendulous, fleshy sacks. Many Jafa women find this hard to accept and spiral into a deep depression, convinced they will never again be able to compete with other image-conscious Jafas.

There is no known cure for PND, which statistics show affects Jafa women disproportionately. The only recognised treatment yet developed is expensive — a pair of Italian designer shoes worth at least $500 to be taken soon after birth. Unfortunately this treatment is not always effective as foot swelling often prevents the shoes being administered.

Raising the Jafa

DEALING WITH THE 'APRÈS BIRTH'

Some people favour burying the afterbirth (known as 'après birth' among Jafas). This is a symbolic gesture expressing the cycle of life. However, an increasingly popular trend among Jafas is to have a local artist use the afterbirth to paint an abstract work of art. The painting is intended to symbolise beauty, life and just how lucrative investing in art can be. The work may later adorn a Jafa's hallway or bedroom or be sold at an art auction (as long as it has been allowed to dry properly).

PRESERVING THE MOMENT FOR POSTERITY

With today's camcorders it is easier than ever to capture the moment of truth on video. Once you've recorded the moment of conception you can begin to think about how you might like to immortalise the moment your child enters Auckland. In true Jafa circles it is not acceptable for the home movie of your child's birth to exist simply as a record of the event. It must also possess artistic merit. Many Jafas now routinely hire **television commercial directors** to bring a strong visual style to the presentation of their births. If the film is a success it can even be entered into several overseas film festivals. The short film of **Petra Bagust**'s home birth recently won the prestigious *Golden Bassoon* at the Copenhagen International Short Film Festival.

WHAT IF YOUR CHILD IS 'DIFFERENT'?

All parents hope their child will be healthy and normal but what do you do if your child is born different? With any birth there is always a risk your child will be born **ugly** — perhaps the most feared outcome for Jafa parents hoping to raise a child in Auckland. Sadly, modern technology cannot predict the onset of ugliness (all foetuses appear ugly in ultrasound testing). One in six babies exhibit ugly tendencies and one in 10 are afflicted with full-blown ugliness. Although an ugly child presents a huge challenge for parents, there is no reason why those affected can't live relatively normal lives in Jafa society. As soon as the child is old enough to realise it is different the parents should make sure that the child understands it is 'special' and point out that it can still do all the things other kids do, just alone and well away from where anyone else can see. Choosing the right school for the child is important. There are special schools in places like Hamilton and Levin that specialise in ugly children.

MY CHILD WAS BORN UGLY: JACKIE'S STORY

When we found out Geoffrey was ugly our first concern was how he would fit in. Would our good-looking, well-bred friends' children accept him? It didn't help that I was too embarrassed to show him to my Jafa friends who all seemed to have such beautiful children. I was scared of being judged a failure for producing a child bereft of even reasonable good looks. But then I realised there was no point hiding the truth. In the end my friends were understanding. Everyone encouraged me to have more kids — they were convinced I could improve on my first effort. Now Geoffrey's doing really well, especially since the extensive facial reconstructive surgery.

NAMING YOUR CHILD

A child's name is something it will have to live with for the rest of its life. Jafas therefore tend to choose names they believe are 'timeless'. All Jafa children are named after one of the following:

Precious stones —	Continents or countries —	European places —
Ruby	Asia	Paris
Pearl	Africa	Nice
Jewel	India	Tuscany
Michael Hill	Gondwanaland	Bosnia

When thinking of a Jafa name for your Jafling consider the following starters:
- The city in which the child was conceived (provided your child was conceived in Europe);
- The continent or country whose suffering children you feel the most empathy for;
- The European province that inspired the décor of your second bathroom.

NAMES TO AVOID

Jafas tend to steer well clear of any name that is the same as a New Zealand town or place because these are meaningless to Jafas, for example:

Nelson	Rodney	Russell
Martin	Shirley	Otorohanga

JAFA NAMES ON THE RISE

Auckland's changing ethnic profile has influenced the names most commonly given to the city's newest Jafas. The most popular include:

미희자

滿仔

जगदीप

Jeff the Jafa says:
'We wanted to name our daughter after that special miracle that helped make her possible, so we called her Viagra.'

CAN I BREASTFEED EVEN THOUGH I HAVE IMPLANTS?

Many Jafa mothers worry that their breast implants may interfere with breastfeeding. There is no reason why a mother with implants can't lactate normally and therefore breastfeed her child. The biggest problem is the discomfort likely to result when the breasts become heavily engorged and the milk mixes with the saline solution contained by the implants. Thankfully this poses no threat to the implants, although the baby may appear bloated and can have serious health problems in later life.

THE FOUR-WHEEL-DRIVE PRAM

Jeep recently realised its Jeep four-wheel-drive pram. Now Jafa kids can establish class distinctions, just like Jafa adults.

RAISING A BABY GAY

Childless Jafa homosexual couples may choose to adopt children. Raising a baby gay presents its own challenges (for more on this see Gunter Hurst's landmark work *Raising a Gayby*). Briefly though, the most important issue will likely be ensuring the child enjoys a balanced upbringing in terms of its gender influences. If the child is exposed to equal measures of masculine and feminine influence it should turn out roughly like **John Campbell** (with a 2–3 per cent variation in levels of camp).

GAY DOGS: THE NEW SURROGATE CHILDREN

Many gay Jafas prefer domesticated pets to children and will adopt dogs as surrogate children. As a surrogate a **pedigree dog** offers many advantages over a baby, for example:

- A dog is more loyal than an infant;
- A dog can hear higher-pitched noises;
- If a dog gets run over, you can just buy a new one.

Of course there are disadvantages, too. A dog is more likely than an infant to auto-fellate or eat its own faeces in front of guests and even a well-trained animal could literally murder your neighbour's cat. When raising a dog as a surrogate child, choose a diminutive breed that can be pampered and spoilt just like a child. Don't be afraid to 'cross the species barrier' by bathing it in the kitchen sink and/or technically snogging it by letting it lick your lips.

Babies have a natural appeal, even to Jafas, which dogs cannot match, so any canine surrogate child must be **extremely cute** to compete. Improve the cuteness of your surrogate-child-dog by dressing it as though it were a child with bows, ribbons and custom-made jackets for special occasions such as weddings, funerals and coming-out parties.

ADOPTING

Many Jafas, particularly cash-rich but time-poor Jafas, favour adoption because it allows them to acquire a child instantly and without damage to expensively toned bodies. It also means that even those couples who refuse to sleep together can start a family. Most Jafas like to consider underprivileged children when adopting. Being staunchly fair-minded and equality-conscious, Jafas will never select a child for adoption on criteria of race, religion or creed but on grounds of **fashionability**. Where the child comes from will depend on which bloody ethnic conflicts are in vogue at any given time. A child from any region that has had a rock concert held to benefit it is ideal. There are a number of agencies that help Jafa couples adopt these **war babies** and specialise in matching a child to a couple and their décor.

TOP FOUR JAFA-PREFERRED LOCATIONS FOR ADOPTION			
Iraq	Afghanistan	Chechnya	West Auckland

SPONSORING A CHILD

For many Jafas, the idea of actually having a real child in their house is abhorrent, but as couples who choose childlessness can be considered selfish, cold and heartless, many decide to sponsor an African child instead. This way they can appear caring and charitable, without actually risking the walls of their villa being scuffed by a marauding infant.

GETTING THE MOST OUT OF YOUR AFRICAN CHILD — SOME POINTERS

CHOOSING AN AFRICAN CHILD

In Auckland, appearances are everything. Insist on the type of child sponsor agency that provides monthly photos of the underprivileged child you are sponsoring. These photos can be framed and displayed prominently on the mantelpiece of your Jafa living room for maximum visibility.

When first joining a sponsorship scheme, ask to view a selection of eligible children and pick one that looks needy and desperate but is also suitably cute. It is also common in these schemes for a child to send you their drawings. Once you have chosen a child ask for a portfolio of its work. It's important that they have at least some level of artistic flair so that their work will compliment the other art in your home. The name of the sponsored child is also important. The more ethnic the name, the more it stands out in conversation, therefore children in Africa with names like Mkhaya or Matabumbi are a better option than ones called Simon or Elaine.

SHOWING YOU REALLY CARE

Many Jafas take this kind of charity very seriously, which is why some Jafa child sponsors like to go the extra mile and give more than the mandatory $1-or-so a day. Some give $2 every Friday and encourage the child to take a friend out to dinner. Some sponsorship agencies discourage this, fearing that giving extra to your sponsored child might make other sponsored children jealous. However, many agencies are happy to pass on small gifts. Be sure any gift you select for your starving child is appropriate to the child's culture, belief and geographical location.

PROMOTE YOUR BRAND OVERSEAS

Because you are sponsoring an African child you can expect to enjoy the same privileges as any other sponsor. Your child can be expected to wear any sponsored clothing you may provide, including caps and polo shirts emblazoned with your family name or the name of your business. Make it clear that your starving child is obligated to wear these at all public appearances.

Raising the Jafa

These African children were delighted to receive a gift from their Jafa sponsors.

THE $1000-A-DAY CHILDREN — SAVING UNDERPRIVILEGED JAFAS FROM ADVERSITY

After the terrible losses of the stock market crashes in 1987 and 2000 it was discovered that Auckland's so-called 'rich Jafas' were significantly less well off than their overseas counterparts. The middle to upper-middle classes' standard of living had dropped considerably and many adolescents, particularly in the central suburbs, were forced to go without everyday necessities like satellite phones, basic Gucci eye protection and gold cards. Many families had to subdivide their estates and thus faced the indignity of having to share a driveway with others. Unable to afford proper clothes, those worst hit were forced to wear last year's fashions. The social impact was immediate. Divorce rates fell and the level of white-collar crime skyrocketed.

In response, a radical new scheme was launched to lift the Jafa standard of living to the bare minimum recommended by the Business Round Table. The '$1000-a-Day Scheme' took impoverished Jafa youth and placed them with 'sponsor' families. 'For just $1000 dollars a day, or the price of a Louis Vuitton overnight bag, you can help boys like Jeremy turn his stock portfolio around,' ran the publicity.

The scheme was a huge success. Sponsorship helped pay for much-needed medical services to fight preventable diseases like gout. It also provided much-needed surgical procedures such as breast augmentation and facelifts. Although the standard of living in suburbs like Remuera is still considered Third World when compared to Beverley Hills, the $1000-a-Day Scheme has helped restore dignity to a once-proud part of the city.

RAISING A JAFLING — THE EARLY YEARS

The first 24 months is a crucial period in a young Jafa's life. This will see the Jafling develop a sense of their own Jafaness, as well as an understanding of what it is to be a Jafa. The following is a guide to some of the milestones a Jafa infant should reach along the way.

JAFA CHILD-REARING GUIDE TO DEVELOPMENTAL MILESTONES

THE FIRST YEAR

1   MONTH —Your Jafa child is weighed and measured to confirm it is a baby.

2   MONTHS — Your Jafa infant achieves 'self-awareness', or in the case of advanced Jafaness, self-importance.

3   MONTHS — If your Jafa child is female she may have already mastered basic multi-tasking allowing her to simultaneously soil her nappy and projectile vomit while eating sand licked up off Mum's imported ornamental zen garden in the conservatory.

4   MONTHS —Your Jafa child should now be able to support its head and maintain focus for short periods – time for its first Anne Geddes calendar shoot (save on child portraits while increasing your child's profile). Anne Geddes can help your child foster important skills such as the ability to work with the camera and the ability to sit up and balance in a massive, hollowed-out pumpkin.

5   MONTHS —Your Jafa child should now have mastered basic motor skills such as the ability to work the cigarette lighter in the 4X4 and brand the family Dalmatian with it.

6   MONTHS — Your Jafa infant can be weaned off breast milk and onto café milk by taking its first espresso Fluffy.

7   MONTHS —Your Jafa child is now crawling. Time to consider a crawl-in wardrobe.

8   MONTHS — There are usually no milestones reached at eight months (if your Jafa child does achieve a milestone immediately consult your doctor as this could be a case of hypermilestonitis).

9   MONTHS — Your Jafa child is examined to determine its medically 'best side'. From now on the child should only be photographed from this side in order to achieve the most flattering results.

10 MONTHS — Time to think about 'total immersion' options for making your child multilingual. Consider a family trip to Tuscany.

11 MONTHS — Child is now old enough to begin seeing a Life Coach, mother begins to scale back her involvement with the child to just using it as a fashion accessory.

12 MONTHS — Jafa child should now be old enough to recognise and judge other children by the model and brand of their strollers.

Raising the Jafa

THE SECOND YEAR

Like any toddler, at around 24 months the infant Jafling will enter a period often lamentably referred to as 'the terrible twos' or, in the case of Jafas, 'the terrible two to twenty-twos'. This phase affects Jafa behaviour from two years of age right through until they leave for their OE. It is a time of discovery when the young Jafa learns that they can demand what they want, ignore the wants and needs of others and just generally not care. Typical behaviour during this difficult time may progress from screaming fits to general rudeness to a seemingly preternatural arrogance and eventually a propensity to run over little old ladies' cats in late-model Porsches.

LEARNING LANGUAGES

Well-raised Jafa children are brought up to be multilingual from an early age. Auckland children must be able to speak English (Jafanese), French and Italian as a bare minimum. Romance languages are essential because children need to be able to get by if New Zealand is ever invaded by the French or

Jen the Jafa says:
'We've started our child on algebra and French but she finds it hard to focus. I think she might be teething.'

Italians (as occurred during the America's Cup) and also so that they can impress at dinner parties in later life. A general knowledge of Maori pronunciation is also advisable in order to impress foreigners (you should aim to have your child's pronunciation at least five times better than most Maori by the age of nine).

JAFA GUIDE TO MAORI PRONUNCIATION

Word	Kiwi Pronunciation	Maori Pronunciation	Jafa Pronunciation
Taupo	Tao-poe	Toe-por	Tooor-pooor
Kaumatua	Old fogie	Koe-ma-too-ah	Kowww-maaaa-tooo-ahhhh
Maori	Mar-ree	Mow-ree	Mouldy
Kia ora	Kee-oora	Kiow-ra	Keeo-ohww-ra
Haere mai	Hoy-ree-moy	Ha-reh-my	Ciao!!!
Te Awamutu	Tee-a-moo-do	Tay-a-wa-mu-tu	No, never heard of it, sorry.

Young Jafas are indoctrinated into the Auckland way of life early. These youngsters are attending a Wendy house auction.

EXPLAINING THE FACTS OF LIFE JAFA-STYLE

This is a difficult task for any parent. It is important to prepare for and come to terms with the inevitable loss of innocence that is going to occur when your child educates you about sexual acts you never knew existed. Naturally you'll be taken aback by how much your child has already learnt in the playground and from Britney Spears videos but once you've overcome the initial shock of learning what 'frot-balling' is, you can get on with educating your child about the realities of human reproduction. When it comes to the birds and the bees, be perfectly frank and honest with your Jafling. A matter-of-fact account is the best way for the adolescent to gain an understanding of the wider importance of sex in Jafa life. Consider the reconstruction below:

JAFA ADOLESCENT: Daddy, where do I come from?
JAFA FATHER: Auckland, and don't you forget it.

Raising the Jafa

JAFA ADOLESCENT: No, I mean where *did* I come from? How are babies made?

JAFA FATHER: Oh. Well, just like any other mistake — by accident.

JAFA ADOLESCENT: Yeah, but how?

At this point the Jafa father should shift uncomfortably in his designer armchair, which, even though it cost $5000, is not actually that comfortable.

JAFA FATHER: All right then.

At this point the child should be taken onto the father's knee and the father may start a pipe (optional).

JAFA FATHER: Well, son, sometimes a man meets a woman and decides he 'likes' the woman and wants to 'like' her even more, preferably at least three times a week. So the man asks the woman to spend time with him and she agrees because, even though the man resembles Rodney Hyde, at the end of the day he drives a 2004 model 6 series BMW.

JAFA ADOLESCENT: Who's Rodney Hyde?

JAFA FATHER: Never mind. So the man and the woman spend time together and...

JAFA ADOLESCENT: Like you and Mummy?

JAFA FATHER: No, like Mummy and I used to spend time together, before you turned up. Remember, this is just the theory.

JAFA ADOLESCENT: Sorry.

JAFA FATHER: So the man and the woman spend time together and eventually, when the man has spent approximately two-thirds of his disposable income on the woman, the woman lets the man rub up against her.

JAFA ADOLESCENT: Wow.

JAFA FATHER: I know.

PAUSE

JAFA ADOLESCENT: Is it like how Cujo rubs up against your leg sometimes?

JAFA FATHER: Exactly. Well, not exactly, but you're on the right track. Anyway, to make a long story short, the man rubs up against the woman in a very special way and eventually he experiences sensations of intense euphoria...

JAFA ADOLESCENT: Like you had when Auckland took the Shield off Canterbury?

JAFA FATHER: No, not that good. I'm thinking more of very nice feelings, like when you're about to sneeze but not quite and then you do. Anyway, at this point the man releases millions of tiny fish-like creatures into the woman.

JAFA ADOLESCENT: Wow.

JAFA FATHER: I know, especially as the man promised he'd pull out but never did. Anyway, the fish...

JAFA ADOLESCENT: Orange Roughy?

JAFA FATHER: No, smaller.

JAFA ADOLESCENT: Undersized?

JAFA FATHER: Don't worry about the size of the fish, the point is the fish eat eggs and then turn into something made of ultrasound. This eventually turns into a baby, which grows inside the woman and pops out a few months later to wreak havoc on both the man's and the woman's life. That's how babies are made son. Any questions?

JAFA ADOLESCENT: No, seems pretty straightforward; it just involves Rodney Hyde, a BMW and some fish.

JAFA FATHER: Right, but not necessarily in that order.

JAFA TEENS

At around 14 years of age it is perfectly normal for an adolescent to become obnoxious, arrogant and self-centred, or in the case of the Jafa adolescent, more so. Don't worry, this is just a phase that usually passes by the age of 70.

SCHOOLING

There are many schools of thought on how children's thought should be schooled. The main issue for the Jafa is whether to go with public or private education.

PUBLIC OR PRIVATE EDUCATION?

As a general rule, private is always superior to public — in anything. For example, private transport beats public transport, while only certain individuals and George Michael prefer public toilets to private ones. Similarly, public schools are inherently inferior to their private counterparts. According to the *Way of the Jafa*, a private school is a young Jafa's ticket to higher education and a higher paying job in the corporate world. Expensive cars and country clubs follow naturally. Public schools, on the other hand, will almost certainly lead to teenage pregnancy, drug abuse, unemployment and prostitution.*

These public-school kids seem happy, but sadly their chances of owning
their own PR firm before the age of 12 are
less than half that of any school kid in a tartan uniform.

CHOOSING THE RIGHT SCHOOL — WHAT TO LOOK FOR

APPRAISE THE SCHOOL UNIFORM

A good Jafa school's uniform should involve one or all of the following: caps, stripes and tartan. If it's a girls' school the uniform should be no

* Although this is a stereotype, it is 100 per cent true.

more than mildly sexy to middle-aged men. A good school uniform will usually indicate a good school with better opportunities. Consider the examples below:

Good Jafa school uniform.   Bad school uniform.

CONSIDER SCHOOL ZONES

A school zone is a magical force field surrounding a school that enriches all the homes under its influence, enhancing their value. Think of this as the school's 'aura' and look for a school with a good aura. Some school zones are more powerful than others. The Auckland Grammar School zone, for instance, has been known to affect property values in Hamilton.

CONSIDER THE SCHOOL MOTTO

It doesn't matter what it means or if it even makes sense — as long as it's in Latin it's a good school.

CONSIDER THE TEACHERS

A good teacher should, as a bare minimum, have a degree (of decorum, if not a BA). Ask to be taken to the staffroom so you can get some idea of what the teachers are like. Do they look interested in their work? Can they spell their own names? Are any of them being led away in handcuffs by undercover police officers?

DEVOTIONAL SCHOOLS

Private religious schools have to charge their students higher fees because of the increased operating costs resulting from their large grounds, older buildings and the legal expenses of having to defend child molestation charges against their brethren. Many Jafa parents are nonetheless willing to pay these higher fees because devotional schools offer religious guidance. This normally takes the form of beatings. Corporal punishment is still widely regarded as the most effective way to get children to appreciate a Christian approach to life. Private schools in this mould have also proven that religiously schooled students do well, especially when they fear they will burn in hell if they do anything wrong.

Another advantage of religious schools is that many provide a boarding option. Jafa parents can send their children away, safe in the knowledge that their offspring will receive a 24-hour education not limited to the classroom or the hours of daylight.

Detractors like to compare boarding schools to prisons but in reality their food is not that good. At private schools young Jafas learn things that are not taught at public schools. For example:

Girls learn how to:
- sneeze without actually sneezing;
- exit a car without doing a 'Sharon Stone' (AKA 'Rachel Hunter');
- preserve one's virginity until the last possible moment;
- remove a bra through clothes.

Boys learn how to:
- remove a bra through clothes;
- form old boys' networks;
- achieve an erection at the bottom of a collapsed scrum.

A BRIEF GUIDE TO AUCKLAND'S TOP PRIVATE SCHOOLS

AUCKLAND GRAMMAR SCHOOL

Grammar has produced more **All Blacks** and New Zealand representative cricketers than any other New Zealand school, which just goes to show that **corporal punishment** works not just as a means of sexual gratification but as an educational tool as well.

SAINT CUTHBERT'S

Besides its outstanding academic record, Saint Cuthbert's has a fine sporting heritage, having produced more **All Blacks' wives** than any other girls' school.

THREE QUEENS COLLEGE

Three Queens College is one of Auckland's most exclusive private boarding schools and has always prided itself on being on the cutting edge of **educational technologies**. In 1993 it became the first school to issue each student with a laptop computer. This policy is currently under review, however, after it was discovered that the third-form boys had been running a lucrative Internet porn site for seven years.

SAINT KENTIGERN'S

One of Auckland's more exclusive schools, Saint Kentigern's is most famous for its **extra-curricular activities** and school trips. Each year the school sends its sixth-form Art History class to Italy and next year the seventh-form Physics class plans to send three boys to the moon as part of the school space programme.

11 TRANSPORTING THE JAFA
GETTING AROUND IN AUCKLAND

PUBLIC AND OTHER TRANSPORT

Aucklanders regard public transport in the same way they regard public toilets — as something that should only be used in the case of an emergency and so long as no one sees them using it. Nonetheless, Auckland does have a public transport system — it's called the motorway. But there are other ways of failing to get anywhere on time in Auckland.

WAY OF THE JAFA

TAXIS

New Zealand's immigration policy has succeeded in bringing some of the world's most skilled professionals to our shores. Most can't get jobs in their chosen field and end up driving cabs, which means Auckland now boasts **the Southern Hemisphere's most over-qualified taxi driver fleet**. As many as 12 per cent of Auckland's taxi drivers are actually astronauts, which may explain their inability to control a vehicle subject to gravity. Most Jafa cabbies are actually doctors and engineers whose qualifications aren't recognised in New Zealand. While this can mean taxis are not the best mode of transport in Auckland, they are an ideal option for having a baby or seeking advice on a major engineering project. Many Jafa mothers elect to have **cab births** because Auckland's foreign cab-driving doctors are better qualified than local doctors and often more awake.

Rajev Patel — former UN Ambassador for India and winner of the Nobel Peace Prize.

FROM DEREGULATION TO RE-REGULATION

In 1996 the Auckland City Council established laws to regulate the city's taxi drivers. The 'Taxi Warrant of Fitness Scheme' was introduced. To maintain their licence, cabbies must now be able to locate key Auckland landmarks such as the Sky Tower, the ocean and the median strip. The new scheme also ensures that cabs are not polluting the environment by testing the drivers' emissions.

BUSES

Auckland's buses have long been saddled with a reputation for being infrequent, unreliable and erratic but improvements have been made. Since the introduction of compulsory wheel alignment they have been less erratic. Auckland's most popular bus service is **The Link**, so called because it is the only known link between Auckland and the possibility of a vaguely functioning public transport system.

Auckland buses are among the most polite in the world.
This one is on its way to West Auckland.

Getting a seat on an Auckland bus can be difficult —
there are just so many to choose from.

WAY OF THE JAFA

Like wild dogs, Auckland's buses tend to travel in packs or small convoys or not at all. Indeed, buses are so infrequent on Auckland roads that even runaway coaches have been pursued and boarded by desperate commuters. Another problem has been **crime**. In the rougher parts of the city, drivers often refuse to stop to pick up passengers and may even refuse to stop for red lights. To find out about bus timetables, and if they plan to publish any, call Busline on 09 366640509.

HOW TO SIGNAL A JAFA BUS DRIVER

Jump repeatedly on the spot waving your arms frantically. This will cause the driver to speed up and look the other way, pretending he hasn't seen you. Now is your chance! Scatter nails or broken glass on the road. These will rupture the bus's tyres and cause it to stop. It may not be operational again for quite some time, but having waited two hours, what's another two?

TRAINS

Auckland's rail system was known as 'cutting edge' for many years, mainly because of the number of severed limbs resulting from industrial accidents on the tracks. It is not recommended for visitors to Auckland to take a train, unless they intend to turn it to some useful purpose.

BRITOMART

The jewel in the Auckland public transport crown is undoubtedly yet to be built, but in the meantime the city is making do with Britomart, a state-of-the-art transport hub or **white elephant** as it is technically known.

Britomart was the brainchild of the Auckland City Council. The fact that its brainchild was stillborn has not detracted from this remarkable achievement. A multimillion-dollar investment resulted in the best design, construction and positioning for the rail and bus station, and true to the council's promise Britomart did not want for anything, except trains. It takes only one visit to realise that Britomart has been cleverly designed to strongly resemble a **giant gay nightclub**. This is so it can easily be converted when it fails in the purpose for which it was intended.

Auckland train timetables are so unreliable, most Jafas tend to rely on more traditional methods of predicting arrivals.

CYCLING

Cycling is a good means of transport in Auckland. Many Jafas will take a bike around the city, usually by attaching it to the roof rack of their 4X4. Until recently there was a serious problem with the number of cyclists being run down by cars in the inner city. The creation of dedicated bus/bike lanes has alleviated this problem. However, the number of cyclists run over by buses is up 38 per cent.

WAS A JAFA THE FIRST TO FLY?

It's a little-known fact but a Jafa was probably the first person to attempt **powered flight**. George Bolte, better known as 'Happy Jackles', was a Victorian turn-of-the-century circus clown whom many claim beat the Wright Brothers in getting airborne. Tapping his knowledge of old-time clowning, Bolte used a few whittled tent poles and the canvas from his massively baggy pants to fashion a crude fuselage. His outrageously massive shoes were hollowed out to act as wings while his heavily starched spinning bow tie served as a propeller. Historians say Bolte was years ahead of his time in understanding that a comically small toy plane powered by pedals almost too small for a man to turn would be lighter and therefore more likely to fly. Hundreds gathered under the Wringo Brothers' Big Top on 22 March 1903 to witness 'Happy Jackles' Magnificient Airborne Antics'. It was to be one of the world's first attempts at powered flight. Eyewitness accounts suggest Bolte twice became airborne in his wacky machine. However, it crashed into a wall and was incinerated, making it the world's first powdered flight.

Was this clown the first man to fly?

PARKING

Parking in Auckland is often described as a 'nightmare' but it is not quite that good. Cars deemed illegally parked are immediately towed and impounded. While this is inconvenient, it is sometimes the only way to actually get your car into a park in Auckland. Parking rates are reasonable out of the city where the hourly rate is about $2 but can be expensive in the central city where the hourly rate is about the same as a good lawyer. The revenue collected by parking wardens is channelled back into parking — it helps pay for the Parking Division's end-of-year Christmas party in Fiji.

In Auckland, Jafa parking wardens have the authority to give tickets for failure to display a warrant of fitness, failure to display registration and failure to display wealth.

DISABLED PARKING

Disabled motorists are well catered for in Auckland with special parking dispensation provided close to most essential amenities (shopping, schools, pubs). However, with the parking situation being so dire, many groups are now lobbying to have their disabilities officially recognised so that they, too, can enjoy disabled parking privileges. These groups include those disabled by impotence, dyslexia, xenophobia and living in Hamilton.

AUCKLAND TRAFFIC

The first thing that many people notice about Auckland is that everyone is in a hurry to get somewhere. In Auckland, even those with nowhere to go are in a hurry to get to where they don't need to be. Ironically, the people in the biggest hurry are always moving at the slowest rate. The technical term for this phenomenon is **traffic**. The focal point of Auckland's traffic is its state-of-the-art motorway system, where people with a common interest in getting somewhere quickly come together to ensure that this remains an impossibility for everyone. Statistics tell us that the average Aucklander spends up to three years of their life waiting at stop signs, four years waiting at traffic lights and more than six years looking for a park — often just the one. Nonetheless Jafas love theirs cars because they represent freedom — the freedom to get into your car at any time and drive straight into a traffic jam.

Jen the Jafa says:
'I have a mantra that keeps me calm in traffic. I just slowly and clearly repeat it to myself: "GET THE F**K OUT OF MY WAY!"'

Jafas adore their cars. Although they favour larger models such as 4X4s, it is not uncommon for a Jafa to own a small car — this is used to drive them from their bigger car to the front door of their house.

When first planned in the 1950s, Auckland's motorways were among the first
to employ the revolutionary 'bottleneck' design.

DRIVING ON THE MOTORWAY

Auckland's motorway is undoubtedly the best car park in the city so driving
on it can be a challenge. The most important thing to remember when driving
on Auckland's motorway is NOT USING YOUR INDICATOR. Flashing
indicators are so rarely seen in Auckland that they have been known to
dazzle motorists, causing serious accidents such as normal traffic flow.

ADVANTAGES OF THE AUCKLAND MOTORWAY SYSTEM

- It's a system, if only by name.
- Relationships can be formed with people stuck next to you on the motorway.
- Provides an excellent opportunity to sit back, relax and really enjoy a good bumper sticker.

DISADVANTAGES OF THE AUCKLAND MOTORWAY SYSTEM

- It's a system, if only by name.
- Relationships can be formed with people stuck next to you on the motorway.
- Provides an excellent opportunity to sit back, relax and really enjoy a good bumper sticker.

CELLPHONE USE WHILE DRIVING

Cellphone use while driving, such as text messaging, is not usually a problem for the female Jafa because of her ability to multi-task. For Jafa men (whose idea of multi-tasking is groping a woman's breast at the same time as kissing her) the prospect is more challenging. While dangerous, there are advantages to texting while driving; if you're approaching an intersection and you're not sure who has right of way, you can text a friend and ask them; if your texting causes an accident, at least you are already on the phone, allowing you to contact emergency services that much quicker. Even if you die in an accident as a result of texting while driving, at least your last act on Earth makes you look popular and 'with it'.

FOUR WAYS TO KILL TIME IN AN AUCKLAND TRAFFIC JAM

1. Replace fluffy dice with Rubik's cube.
2. Call talkback radio on your mobile and raise the issue of Auckland's traffic problem.
3. In winter, use your vehicle's climate-control mechanism to fog up the windows then amuse yourself by tracing crude renditions of genitalia with your index finger.
4. Using your cellphone, hack into the police central computer to access the overhead electronic signs that hang over the motorway. Amuse yourself by typing out your own messages for motorists. For example: 'Beep if you think this sucks,' or 'I put a bomb on that bus!'

AUCKLAND'S ROAD CODE

JAFA ROAD RULES — A BASIC GUIDE

The two basic rules that must be observed on the roads of Auckland at all times are as follows:

1. Give way to all vehicles coming from your right, unless someone is trying to get in front of you, in which case give way to your emotions.
2. Signal for at least three seconds, longer if you're really angry.

Jeff the Jafa says:
'Aucklanders go on about how bad our immigrant drivers are. They're not any worse at driving than us; they're just better at having accidents.'

Auckland has several exceptions to the standard New Zealand road code. The most important are illustrated below.

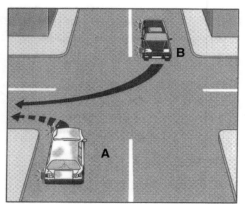

New Zealand Road Code says:
Car A gives way to Car B because you must give way to all cars approaching from your right.

Jafa Road Code says:
Car B has right of way because the combined cost of its tyres is greater than the yearly wage of the driver of Car A.

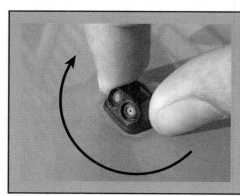

HOW TO DEAL WITH WINDSCREEN WASHERS AT TRAFFIC LIGHTS

Windscreen washers will often sneak up on Jafa motorists at traffic lights and begin washing their windscreens in hope of gold coins. You can guard against this by turning your windscreen cleaner fluid jets outwards. When the windscreen washer makes an unwarranted approach, activate the windscreen washer jets. The stinging cleaner fluid will momentarily blind your assailant, allowing you to escape at the next change of lights.

JAFAS AND THEIR CARS

THE RISE AND RISE OF THE 4X4 JEEP OR SUV (SPORTS UTILITY VEHICLE)

The most popular Jafa car is unquestionably the 4X4 Jeep or SUV (Sports Utility Vehicle), also known as the Remuera Tractor. The 4X4 offers the promise of increased safety on Auckland roads. Jafas find it reassuring that, in the event of an accident, not only will they be safely preserved, the other car will be completely destroyed.

ADVANTAGES OF THE JEEP/4X4/SUV/REMUERA TRACTOR TO A JAFA

- Relatively cheap to run (when compared to an aircraft carrier);
- Has enough room to store even the biggest ego;
- Increased elevation means you can better see traffic and, on a clear day, Mount Ruapehu;
- Massive tyres allow the Jafa to run over cats, dogs and other vehicles without even noticing, thus sparing them any feelings of guilt or remorse;
- Allows the Jafa to look down on the person at the drive-thru window (which 'feels more right').

ARE SUVS REALLY THAT MUCH SAFER?

While the size of SUVs is often associated with increased safety there are many related problems. The interior proportions of popular Jafa SUVs have reached such a scale that even large objects are easily lost in the back seat. In January 2002 a search party of concerned accountants combed Parnell for two missing boys who were eventually discovered living in a 'Lord of the Flies'-type society in the back of their family's Land Rover.

A Jafa woman typically prefers her SUV to be as large as possible because the bigger the vehicle, the thinner she will look next to it. By the same logic the most popular colour is black.

LITTLE-KNOWN SUV SAFETY ISSUES

ECHO

The interior of the average Jafa SUV is so spacious that echoing can be a problem. The sound of the SUV driver's own voice can bounce back at them causing disorientation. Equally, music can echo almost indefinitely making it impossible to hear the car horns of other cars or the shouts of their drivers.

AIR QUALITY

SUV drivers prize the SUV's superior height, claiming this helps them 'look over' traffic (in fact, research suggests they are more likely to 'overlook' other traffic). However, Jafa SUVs are now so high that oxygen levels at the driver's altitude are significantly lower than at sea level. The paucity of breathable air has been identified as a contributing factor to impaired judgement and may even induce unconsciousness, particularly of other road users.

Jafas value the four-wheel-drive jeep for its ability to deal with extremely difficult terrain, particularly during shopping excursions.

JAFA SUV MAINTENANCE CHECKLIST

Radiator water	Evian or Perrier mineral water only
Tyre tread	Should be deep enough to house a family of Pygmies
Headlights	Should be bright enough to make other road users think they are about to be abducted by a UFO. There should be at least six sets of headlights, including auxiliary halogen lights, fog lights, rally lights and Christmas lights.
Reverse gear warning tone	Should be loud enough to make the most distant neighbour on your street disconnect his alarm clock.

AN ILLUSTRATED GUIDE TO
JAFA SIGN LANGUAGE FOR THE ROAD

Sign: Elevated central digit.
Meaning: You have right of way.

Sign: Elevated arm with open fist.
Meaning: I have right of way.

Sign: Elevated arm with clenched fist.
Meaning: Who has right of way?

Sign: Right-hand index finger inserted into circle
of left-hand forefinger and thumb, repeatedly.
Meaning: Please slow down.

Sign: Left arm held over elevated right arm,
clenched fist.
Meaning: Please turn your lights on.

Sign: Elevated arm, open hand, fingers spread.
Meaning: I earn five times as much as
you so I go first.

161

12 FEEDING THE JAFA
EATING IN AUCKLAND

Feeding the Jafa can be a difficult job. Sophisticated Aucklanders are very particular about their food. Jafas often adhere to very clear-cut culinary philosophies. The basic Jafa foodie groups can be broken down as follows:

THE REGULAR OMNIVORE

The default culinary setting of most Jafas, the regular omnivore eats anything: meat; vegetables; even sausages, which may contain the lips and anuses of mad-cow diseased cattle — provided the product has the word 'gourmet' in its name.

THE REGULAR VEGETARIAN

Eats only vegetables but can at least talk about meat without vomiting.

THE EXTREMIST VEGETARIAN

Cannot even talk about meat without throwing up bits of carrot and corn. Extremists eat strictly vegetables only and furthermore insist their food must have had no physical or social contact with meat, meat-based products or foodstuffs whose names rhyme with meat. Extremists use vegetarian fridges (which have not seen meat) and can be a problem when entertaining as they may refuse to enter a house that has had meat in it. The extremist's reluctance to wear fur or leather can also create difficulties at B & D parties.

THE VEGAN

The vegan (not to be confused with the Vulcan) eats no animal-derived products whatsoever. Quite often gluten deniers, too, many vegan parents will not allow their children to watch animal-based cartoons such as 'Pingu'. They can kill any dinner party by not revealing their faith until the food is served, a move known as the 'Vegan Death Grip'. While they don't like to admit it, vegans really only eat nuts and berries, making their diet the same as that of a squirrel. The vegan is easily identified by their translucent complexion, pellet-like droppings and telltale inability to draw breath.

ORGANICISTS

Jafa organicists will eat only 'organic' food, i.e. food that specialty stores charge 40 times the going rate for because it is more rotten. Organicists live in fear of agro-chemical contamination. Industrial chemical contamination, on the other hand, is fine — provided it's good Ecstasy and not too 'smacky'.

EATING OUT IN AUCKLAND

Many people complain that in most parts of New Zealand the only food readily available takes the form of $1 meat pies made from reconstituted horse intestines and minced cattle sphincters. Thankfully, the situation in Auckland is a lot more cosmopolitan; where you will pay $8.50 for the same pie. The city boasts a world-class selection of haute cuisine available at some of the **most pretentious and overpriced restaurants in the Southern Hemisphere**.

AUCKLAND RESTAURANT GUIDE BY LOCATION

CENTRAL AUCKLAND

DUBLOVICH'S

Dublovich's is a Russian restaurant that prides itself on serving real Russian food just the way it's served in Russia. The perennial favourite dish is Jzerkevz (potato with salt). Those seeking something more adventurous might try Jzerkevzai (potato with extra salt). Dublovich's is recommended over more commercial 'Russian' eateries that westernise their food by adding extras like sugar, MSG or plates.

Feeding the Jafa

WOTTO'S

Wotto's is a Michelin-rated restaurant famous for its side dishes; these include salads, dips and the waitresses. At Wotto's you can order the **Southern Hemisphere's most expensive salad**, the 'Petit', which consists of two leaves of rocket, one pine nut and a single shaving of Parmesan cheese drizzled in anchovy ejaculate ($64).

The house red at Wotto's has been described as
'bold and brash with fruity overtones',
a description also applied to the waiters.

ESPRESSO LIFE

This boutique café is famous for its exclusive blends of **exotic coffees** imported from South America's most dangerous and inaccessible regions. Sit back and savour a short black, relaxed in the knowledge that several Bolivian peasants died bringing it to you.

NORTH AUCKLAND

ANTONINI'S

Antonini's (named after its flamboyant owner's poodle) is so exclusive that any of the waiters' watches is worth more than the average diner's car. The restaurant is famous for its strict dress code — all diners must wear a dress, even the men. Its impeccable standards make it the domain of an exclusive few, mainly weathly socialites and cross-dressers. The meals here are so expensive Antonini's has its own on-site **personal loan manager**.

THE THIRD WORLD CAFÉ

The Third World Café is an unusual bistro that specialises in **Third World cuisine**. Diners can choose from two kinds of rice gruel served from authentic Red Cross sacks. Customers dine in a traditionally parched sub-Saharan atmosphere with meals served by genuine aid workers who are occasionally kidnapped and beheaded.

THE $2 RESTAURANT

A spin-off of the ever-popular **$2 Dollar Shop** chain, The $2 Restaurant features a wide range of dishes with nothing over $2. This is a good place to come if you're on a budget but not if you're hungry, as the menu consists entirely of side dishes.

EAST AUCKLAND

CHU YUNG FAT'S GRAND HARBOUR DRAGON SEAFOOD BBQ GARDEN RESTAURANT

This intimate, three-level, 600-table buffet restaurant is definitely putting the 'char' back into Yum Cha. Chu Yung Fat's is one of the few Chinese restaurants in Auckland that goes to the trouble of importing its meat directly from China to ensure truly **authentic Chinese cuisine**. Try the famous chicken paws for a real taste of China.

THE DRAG-THRU

The Drag-Thru is the first of a new brand **drive-thru** designed for the 'boy racer' market. Punters move through two cars at a time. The restaurant is located 500 metres from the order box. When the meal is ready drivers get a green light and drag each other to the pick-up. The winner takes all. There is also a designated area of the car park that can be hired for burnouts. Get in quick as the council is already moving to shut down this operation.

SAMURAI SUSHI

Samurai Sushi provides an amazing insight into **traditional Japanese cuisine**. The sashimi is prepared by chefs brandishing actual Samurai blades. The highly exclusive cuisine here is based entirely around the concept of honour. For an extra thrill send your meal back and watch the chef commit Hari-Kari.

Samurai Sushi is the only restaurant in New Zealand where diners can order whale-meat (served for research purposes only).

THE CRIME'N'DINE

The Crime'n'Dine is a dinner theatre restaurant that combines two of West Auckland's favourite obsessions — food and crime. Professional actors perform reconstructions of **unsolved crimes** from the area — it's *Crimewatch* meets an all-u-can-eat buffet. Diners who provide police with helpful information win prizes ranging from meal and movie vouchers to lap dances.

GAZZA'S GROTTO

Gazza's Grotto is Auckland's only underground revolving restaurant. Diners at this converted car park can sample a range of popular dishes whilst marvelling at the intricacy of **underground cabling** up close. There's history here, too; the restaurant passes a series of old unmarked graves dating from colonial times when the area was at the centre of an influenza epidemic. At the time of writing, Gazza's Grotto was not revolving due to a mechanical fault. The restaurant is, however, still open for business, while parts are shipped in from overseas.

FAT ALBERT'S

Henderson's favourite burger restaurant, Fat Albert's opens only occasionally (whenever the owner is out on parole) and when it does it can be hard to get a table (as none are provided) but the food is excellent. Fat Albert's is perhaps most famous for its annual **Bitches Beauty Contest** — the city's only combined Beauty Pageant and Dog Show. West Auckland's prettiest girls and pure-bred attack dogs parade on a stage and make the judges' job difficult, especially as sometimes it's hard to tell who's entered in which part of the contest.

SOUTH AUCKLAND

KFC

Despite a number of modest Chinese restaurants serving traditional Chinese food throughout the area, South Auckland's most popular eatery remains **KFC**. The restaurant on the corner of Great South Road and New South Road manages to be the **busiest KFC in the Southern Hemisphere**, despite being robbed on average twice a week.

THE BATTLE OF VINDALOO CURRY HOUSE

The Battle of Vindaloo claims to serve the **hottest curries in New Zealand**. Many punters come here in the hope of getting 'high on chilli'. All curries are graded by their spiciness from 'Hot' through 'Extra Hot' and 'Ultra Hot,' to 'Molten'. Legend has it that after a plate of the famous Beef Vindaloo it is possible to see through time.

FRIDAY'S SEAFOOD BISTRO

This lively establishment at the mouth of the Manukau Harbour was founded by three recreational fishermen who still supply the restaurant with its **daily catch**. Friday's has continued to maintain a reputation for serving Auckland's freshest undersized fish. A popular spot with seafood lovers, families and MAF officers.

KAIAROHA

A rarity among Auckland dining options, Kaiaroha is the city's only source of **traditional Maori cuisine** boasting a menu based on the diet of pre-European Maori. Diners can choose their own endangered native bird straight from the cage. Unfortunately traditional hangi cooking means the service can be a little slow.

A JAFABETICAL GLOSSARY OF JAFANESE

AA — Acronym for Aucklanders Anonymous, the organisation that runs a 24-hour nervous-breakdown service

AD CREEP — The gradual expansion of advertising space around Auckland into non-traditional areas such as bathroom walls, cars and the every waking utterance of Murray Deaker. Also sometimes used to refer to anyone who works for Saatchi and Saatchi

ADHOCRACY — An organisation without structure or efficiency, e.g. the Auckland City Council

AFFLUARN'T — Term used to refer to Auckland's lower socio-economic groups

AFFLUENZA — A common Jafa health problem whereby an obsession with designer labels leads the sufferer to accumulate critical amounts of credit card debt causing an acute financial health crisis

BARKING HEAD — A broadcaster who appears to have gone barking mad on air, e.g. Paul Holmes

BARKITECTURE — Architecture that is so appallingly ugly one is forced to conclude that the architect who designed it must have been 'barking mad', e.g. Auckland apartment complexes

BLANDIOSE — Very large, utterly bland buildings (see much of downtown Auckland)

BUILDING DISSENT — Making renovations or extensions to a property without first securing consent from the local authorities

CARMA — When a motorist cuts in front of another motorist and is then themselves cut in front of, much to their annoyance

CASHULTY — Damage caused to a Jafa's finances by a major purchase

CARTASTROPHE — A state of affairs in which a Jafa's new hairstyle clashes horribly with the colour or interior of their car

CAR-PET — Vehicle that a Jafa is so attached to it has become like a pet

Jafabetical glossary of Jafanese

CARSONOVA — A Jafa who spends every cent he has on an expensive sports car, which he uses to attract and then bed young women (at their place because he can't afford a house)

CAR-STRATION — The loss of a Jafa's car or driver's licence

CELLPH-ABSORBED — A quality possessed by a Jafa who spends more time engaged with their cellphone at social occasions than with those around them

CELLPH-ESTEEM — The feelings of pride or inferiority that depend on how state-of-the-art your cellphone is

CELLABIT — A Jafa who, on principle, chooses not to have a cellphone

DEPRESSO — A poorly made or bad-tasting espresso coffee

DOOM WITH A VIEW — The state of affairs in which one is doomed to be stuck in traffic at the top of the Auckland Harbour Bridge

EMALE — Male met via the Internet (see also **SPAM** — Emale who turns out to be worthless)

EXT — Particularly irritating text messages from a jilted ex boyfriend/girlfriend/husband/wife

FAIR — The affair you have because you know your partner is having an affair

FOLLOWING DISTANCES — The distance in time it takes the rest of New Zealand to follow the trends set by Aucklanders

GASIAN — Gay Asian immigrant to Auckland whose homosexual credentials are not recognised in New Zealand

GAYBOUR — Gay neighbour

GOOD PERVICE — A state of affairs in which a Jafa restaurant's staff is more delectable than its food

GYMFAMOUS — Someone whose reputation precedes them, but only at Les Mills

JAFLING — A juvenile Jafa, e.g. Paul Holmes

LAY-BORER — A particularly uninteresting sexual partner, usually a young builder or labourer, whom a Jafa woman persists with because he looks good on her arm

MANSCAPING — The artful maintenance of a man's body hair, often by another man

MID-LIFE MOTORCYCLE — A powerful motorcycle, usually a Harley Davidson, bought by a Jafa male going through a mid-life crisis

MID-MID-LIFE CRISIS — The crisis a Jafa male has in the middle of his mid-life crisis when he realises his mid-life crisis is not getting him enough attention

MID-LOVE CRISIS — Running out of Viagra at the most inopportune time

NEGATIVE GEARING — A problem with the Land Rover's transmission

P-CLASS RACING — Endurance racing between P-addicted Jafas to see who can go the longest without sleep (the record of 8 weeks, 2 days and 11 hours set by Ryan Girdworth was later rescinded after it was revealed he had been dead for five of those weeks)

PERSONAL TRAINER — Jafa fitness advisor who makes highly personal comments about your body while you are in compromising stretching positions

PINK-COLLAR WORKER — A member of the Ponsonby hospitality workforce

RETROSEXUAL — Antonym of 'metrosexual'. A Jafa male so archaic in his dress sense and so remiss in his personal hygiene that he appears to be a Neanderthal

ROARING FORTIES — Mid-life crisis years, which see the Jafa male in his forties more socially active than he was in his twenties

SEADUCER — Jafa male who uses his yacht primarily as a prop to lure potential sexual partners

SEXUAL DYSFUNCTION — The act of sleeping with someone your own age

SIX-FIGURE CALORIE — Weight problem

SPAM — Emale who turns out to be worthless

SPEED HUMPS — Casual sex engaged in during a P-binge

SPEED DATING — The act of dating a large number of people in one night because your P-addiction has destroyed your short-term memory

SUBDECISION — The decision on whether or not to subdivide a property

TAN-GERINE — That peculiar shade of orange that results when a Jafa applies excessive amounts of fake tanning lotion

TALKING HEAD — The act of trying to talk whilst performing oral sex, considered bad etiquette among Jafas

TAXIVASION — The act of doing a runner from a taxi without having paid

TIT-TANIC — A Jafa woman whose breast implants are out of proportion to her body size

TRUSTIFARIAN — Trust-fund beneficiary with dreadlocks who lives a fashionably bohemian lifestyle despite having an endless supply of money

UNREAL ESTATE — A nice property in Auckland that is actually affordable

VAGITERIAN — Woman who prefers women

DINING AT THE Y — Act of a woman who prefers women

WELFARIAT — Another name for the populations of South and West Auckland

ABOUT THE AUTHORS

Lee Baker (39) makes his home in Auckland. He lives with his partner Beatrice and at least 14 dogs. He ran guns out of the former Congo in the 1970s before taking up a post with MI5 in Cyprus and then Scotland Yard in Singapore where he helped crack the Mr Asia drug syndicate. After returning to New Zealand he moved into the arts, establishing a reputation as a leading art-house film director. An expert on ancient cultures, Lee is perhaps the world's only anthropologist turned pornographer. His Darwinist film noir *Survival of the Stiffest* (1981) is considered a classic. A recording artist and New Zealand representative cricketer, when not directing films or writing, Lee continues to be one of this country's pre-eminent mountaineers. He is still the only man to have passed wind on each of the world's seven highest peaks in the same calendar year.

As a four-time loser of the Billy T Award for comedy, **Benjamin Crellin** (17) is widely acknowledged as one of New Zealand's top under-achieving comics. His interests outside comedy include collecting rare EFTPOS receipts and science fiction. Benjamin's next literary project will see him complete the first whole translation of *Winnie the Pooh* into Klingon. When not writing Benjamin can usually be seen on stage, where he divides his time between local pub gigs and his annual stand-up comedy tour of North American rest homes.

To find out more about the authors, visit: www.hirsutebooty.com./info/aboutthefounders. Alternatively, take them out and get them really drunk.